Lord, Let Me Walk

A 3-Year Journey With Jesus Through Lent

Weekly Meditations and Activities
on
Christ's Journey to Calvary

Year One: The Year of Becoming
Year Two: The Year of Service
Year Three: The Year of Transformation

by: Susan Grace O'Neill

Susan's website and blog: www.SusanTuttleWrites.com
Email Susan at: aim2write@yahoo.com
Follow Susan on Twitter: @stuttleauthor, Facebook and LinkedIn

Cover design by: Aaron Kondziela (www.aaronkondziela.com)

A WriterWithin Publication
www.WriterWithinPubs.com
ISBN-10: 1-941465-19-6
ISBN-13: 978-1-941465-19-6

Lord, Let Me Walk:
A 3-Year Journey with Jesus through Lent

Weekly Meditations and Activities
on Christ's Journey to Calvary
based on the Catholic Liturgical Readings
for each Sunday of Lent

DEDICATION

This volume is dedicated to four very special women who have graced my life with love, encouragement, support and happiness.

To Sandy Emhof, my "partner in crime" back East, who taught me what true friendship means.

To Brandy McKay, my West Coast "partner in crime," who won't let me get away with anything. This wouldn't have happened without your encouragement.

And to the late Destry Ramey and the late Anna Unkovich, whose courage, love, caring and depth of spirituality continues to awe me every day. How blessed I was to have both of you in my life.

CONTENTS

ACKNOWLEDGMENTS

No one ever writes a book without the help of a lot of other people. I'd like to acknowledge just a few of them here.

After growing up Catholic and attending Catholic schools through college, I roamed a long time without a spiritual home until I stumbled across St. Elizabeth Ann Seton Church in Los Osos, CA. The warmth and peace I found in this small community from the moment I walked through the doors (dragged in, I admit, by my mother when she was visiting me) continues to support and uphold me every day. Each person there is like family to me, but a few stand out:

Previous pastors Fr. Heibar Castañeda and Fr. Lucas Pantoja, and the current pastor, Fr. Joey Buena, are three of the most spiritual and loving priests I've ever met. Their trust and encouragement has made it possible for me to take a deep breath and actually put this into print. Thank you.

My fellow choir members are always there for me: (current) Barbara Mischel, Mark Woehrle, Pete McAdam, Midge LeNoue, Amy Baptiste, Lumen Plunkett, Jane Jaeger, Nicola Morais, and Julia, Christopher and Gabriel Hausser; (past) Julia Long-Meyers, Nellie Corrales and Joe O'Brien. You're the best.

Those I've served with on various committees: Jonniepat

Mobley, Melodianne Duffy, Ron and Mary Munds, the late David Bresnan, Hank Watterworth, Dave and Pat Akey. And of course Javier Soto-Osorio and Heather Hurley, with whom I used to laugh all day when I worked in the parish office; you make work, and life itself, one grand adventure.

Parishioners too numerous to mention: Anne Stewart, Ann Farrelly, Rita Davis, Frank and Elaine Kelley, Lidia McCune, the late Sheila Pouraghabagher, Bill and Maria Jacot, Russell Stimson, Amy and John Baptiste, Albert and Pina Calizo, Carolyn Lemos, and the late Julia Keefe, among so many others, without whom my family would not be complete.

Last, but never least, are my writing friends and mentors at SLO NightWriters and the Central Coast Chapter of Sisters in Crime, the best writing organizations in the world, including Dennis Eamon Young, Janice Konstantinidis, Barbara M. Hodges, Diann Adamson, Rolynn Anderson, Sue McGinty, Marilyn Meredith, and the late Paul Alan Fahey. And especially the Friday Night Writers Group: Debra Davis Hinkle, B. Carter Pittman, Shirley Radcliff Bruton, Christine Taylor, and previous members Jim Leonard, Destry Ramey, Laurie Woodward, and Brandy McKay. Your honesty, encouragement and spiritual depth have helped me be a better writer, and given me the courage to believe enough in myself to bring this out into the world.

And, of course, a huge thank you to my son Aaron Kondziela, the light of my life, my biggest cheerleader, and the brilliant designer of the extraordinary covers for my books. You are, and will always be, the greatest gift God has ever given me.

INTRODUCTION

This journey began years ago when I lived in Angola, New York. I was head of the Liturgy Committee and, along with my best friend, Sandy Emhof, who was head of the folk group, decided to offer the congregation something a little different for Lent, more than the usual Sunday-only presentation.

We brainstormed and came up with the idea of creating a program of sorts, something that Mass-goers could take home and use throughout the week. Based on the colors of the rainbow, it would consist of a new banner each week and an introduction of the week's theme read just before Mass began. Sheets were handed out by greeters as people arrived that included a meditation based on the Mass readings for that day, and activities for each day of the week that helped put the theme into practice.

We had a wonderful time crafting banners that would hang across the back of the church from the choir loft railing. I wrote the introductions and the meditations, and Sandy and I brainstormed the activities. I added a few pertinent quotes from the Book of Proverbs, then typed up and copied sheets to hand out. And wondered what the parishioners would say about our offerings.

The reaction of the congregation that first Sunday of Lent was interesting. Most weren't sure they wanted the sheets because they didn't understand what it was all about. Many who took the sheets did so out of politeness. I saw a lot of confused frowns in the congregation that Sunday; shrugged shoulders and shaking heads until the Lector stood up and read the introduction. Then people began taking another look at the sheets, and at the banner of Christ walking down a path into the wilderness that hung behind them.

By the third week of Lent, congregants actually asked for the meditation sheets as they arrived for Mass. The general consensus was that the meditations and activities brought Lent and Christ's Journey to Calvary home in a very personal way. It seemed to help parishioners see just how very connected we are today to Christ and His glorious Redemption, even though the event occurred two thousand years ago.

They realized it was not a single event that happened in the long-ago past, but a dynamic, personal event that happens now, today, every day, for each and every one of us.

Not until I moved to the Central Coast of California and joined the small but warm and welcoming parish of St. Elizabeth Ann Seton—and joined the music ministry—did I give thought to the Journey I'd written so long ago. I spoke about it to the then pastor, Fr. Heibar Castañeda, who agreed to offer it to the parish for Lent that year. Not until I was looking it over did I realize that the readings were for the wrong cycle. We couldn't use the program as written.

For those who don't know, the readings for Sunday Masses are based on a 3-year cycle in the Catholic Church. Each cycle is different, the readings drawn from various Old and New Testament books and Gospels. To make the Journey program complete, I would need to write the other two cycles, so it could be used by anyone, Catholic or Christian. I took a deep breath, said a heartfelt prayer that God would give me the right words, and sat down to write. This is the result: a 3-year program that takes the reader through Becoming, into Service, and beyond into Transformation. A Journey that mirrors both Christ's life, and His death.

And though the readings are based on the Catholic Cycles, the meditations and activities are broad-based, Biblical, so any Christian can use them. As can those who are seeking connection with Christ and His teachings. This is a Spirit-based program, not a church-based program.

Over the last few years, these Journeys have been used at St. Elizabeth's and other Catholic parishes, by a few local Christian churches and by individuals as well as an inter-faith prayer group on Long Island. They've been used as the base of faith sharing groups, also. I offer them here, to you, and pray that your Journey with Christ will find you in the Light of God's Love, always and forever.

Lord, Let Me Walk

A Journey With Jesus Through Lent

Cycle A:
The Year of Becoming

BIBLICAL READINGS

LORD, LET ME WALK: CYCLE A
THE YEAR OF BECOMING

Week One Color: Red
          Theme: Emotion; Breaking Bonds of Emotion
          Readings:
                  First: Genesis 2: 7-9; 3: 1-7
                  Second: Romans 5: 12-19
                  Gospel: Matthew 4: 1-11

Week Two Color: Orange
          Theme: Pride; Transcending Limitations
          Readings:
                  First: Genesis 12: 1-4a
                  Second: 2 Timothy 1:8b-10
                  Gospel: Matthew 17: 1-9

Week Three Color: Yellow
          Theme: Intellect; Expanding Consciousness
          Readings:
                  First: Exodus 17: 3-7
                  Second: Romans 5: 1-2; 5-8
                  Gospel: John 4: 5-42

Week Four   Color: Green
             Theme: Charity; Finding a New and Wonderful
                                 World
        Readings:
           First: 1 Samuel 16: 1b; 6-7; 10-13a
           Second: Ephesians 5: 8-14
           Gospel: John 9: 1-41

Week Five   Color: Blue
             Theme: Spiritual Obedience; Dormant Talents
                             Come Alive
        Readings:
           First: Ezekiel 37: 12-14
           Second: Romans 8: 8-11
           Gospel: John 11: 1-45

Week Six   Color: Purple
             Theme: Acceptance; Being Better Than You
                      Dreamed You Could Be
        Readings:
           First: Isaiah 50: 4-7
           Second: Philippians 2: 6-11
           Gospel: Matthew 27: 11-54

Easter   Color: White
             Theme: Unity; Inspiration
             Readings:
           First: Acts of the Apostles 10:34a, 37-43
           Second: Colossians 3:1-4
           Gospel: John 20:1-9

LORD LET ME WALK

Journeying with Jesus through Lent
The Year of Becoming: Week One

Life's journey is a process of becoming In-Spirited with our Creator. Coupled with the rainbow as a symbol of ourselves, the six steps we take this year during Lent will lead us into living an In-Spirited life of Unity with God. This first week of our Journey With Jesus, our rainbow color is *red*, the color of *emotion*. Our In-Spiration theme is ***Breaking The Bonds Of Emotion***.

We've all heard the expression, "pushing one's buttons," which means we react on an emotional level to a certain situation, based on things that happened in the past. For example, perhaps our mother or father was critical of us, never pleased no matter how hard we tried. We reacted with rebellion, or anger, or self-loathing, or refusal to continue trying, etc. Now we are grown adults with our own home, our own family. We have, say, a boss who criticizes our efforts. That 'Not Good Enough' button gets pushed again and we react the same way we did as a child. Usually not at work—we can't afford to lose our job—but instead we take it out on our loved ones or friends. Or strangers.

We are all stuck in the past to some degree, emotion-wise. Our 'buttons' get pushed by words or situations that on an unconscious level remind us of a traumatic event in the past, and we react without thinking. We say or do things that we don't really mean.

And afterward we wonder why we reacted the way we did. It wasn't logical, it wasn't mature, it wasn't even the way we wanted to react. Then, when we realize how we've hurt people, we often feel ashamed and unworthy of anyone's friendship or love.

These feelings disconnect us from God. And they maintain the cycle, keeping us stuck in the past, repeating patterns of harmful behavior and negative thinking. The key to breaking the cycle is to discover those 'buttons' of ours that mire us in the past and keep us from moving into Spirit. The best way to begin is to identify what we felt when we reacted badly, and try to remember what was happening when we first felt that way.

But we do not have to deal with our emotions alone. In facing temptation in the desert, our Lord Jesus gave us the tools we need to deactivate our 'buttons' and move back into connection with God. And with peace, serenity, and self-confidence. The tools come from the way Jesus dealt with the devil that tempted Him.

The first step is to **rely on the Word of God** in order to maintain the God-Connection without which we are only half alive. Set aside a few minutes each morning to read the Bible; even a few verses can help us start our day aligned with Spirit.

The second step is to daily **deny the temptation to react without thinking** in thought, word and deed. If we are totally focused on doing and speaking only good, it leaves little room for inappropriate behavior.

And third, **serve only God's desires**, not our own. When we begin to disconnect ourselves from the world, we will find ourselves moving closer and closer to an In-Spirited life.

Let us ask Jesus this week to help us follow the example He set in the desert, in order to shut down the 'buttons' that keep us from finding the In-Spiration of God in our lives. Let us ask Him to help bring the Red of Emotion in our lives into perfect balance with His eternal plan.

NOTE: You may want to start a Year of Becoming Journey With Jesus Journal in which to record your thoughts, prayers, feelings and progress as you Walk With Jesus through Lent. Often, the very act of writing things down makes them more real and a stronger part of our lives. It can also be helpful and enlightening to look back on your journey as the year progresses, and your rainbow continues to grow and shine out to others along their journeys.

Lord, Let Me Walk – Week One Activities

Rainbow Color: Red, the Color of Emotion
Theme of the Week: Breaking Our Bonds To Emotion

THOUGHT FOR THE WEEK

"The strength of a person consists in finding out the way in which
God is going, and going that way, too."
~Henry Ward Beecher

Sunday: Think back on the things that happened to you when
you were a child. Try to identify one or two events that might
have created an emotional 'button.' Then give that 'button' over
to God.

Monday: Focus on speaking and doing only good in every
situation today. (This may not be as easy as you think!)

PROVERBS 10:9 –   "He who walks honestly walks securely, but
he whose ways are crooked will fare badly."

Tuesday: Spend five minutes reading the Bible today. Read
Matthew 4:1-11 (Sunday's Gospel) and think about what Jesus is
really teaching you about yourself.

Wednesday: Talk to someone you don't care for and really listen to them today. Try your best to understand who they are, how they think and feel.

Thursday: Think about what God desires as you do something special for someone. Give them what they really need, not what you want them to need.

PROVERBS 16:3 –   "Entrust your works to the Lord, and your plans will succeed."

Friday: Pray to be open to those with whom you do not agree. Do not argue with anyone today. Let go of anger for just one day.

Saturday: Do something you really don't want to do. As you work at it, consider why you are so reluctant to do it. Does it push a 'button'? Put a name to that feeling, and pray.

PROVERBS 19:21 –   "Many are the plans in a man's heart, but it is the decision of the Lord that endures."

LORD LET ME WALK

Journeying with Jesus through Lent
The Year of Becoming: Week Two

This week our rainbow color is *orange*, which stands for *Pride*, and our In-Spiration theme is *Transcending Limitations*.

Orange is a mixture of red (emotion) and yellow (intellect). Combining them produces orange, which correlates to Pride. Pride has both a positive and a negative aspect. Positive pride opens us up to God and all of His possibilities; negative pride keeps us limited, unbending and focused only on ourselves.

Negative Pride grows into Arrogance. It is based on things of this world—what we accomplish and what we possess. The more we do and the more we have, the more we begin to feel superior to other people.

And it's so easy to feel that way. Today's world praises and rewards material success and material accomplishments with material possessions. Eventually, we come to see ourselves in a worldly light, and base our sense of worth on what we do for a living and what we can buy with the money we earn. We become convinced that we alone know the best way to do things, and hold the only opinion worth listening to. Everything and everyone else is wrong. Worldly pride keeps us narrow, unbending and focused only on ourselves. There is no room for any other options, not even God's.

Positive Pride, or pride that has a spiritual base, becomes Dignity, which consists of honor, humility, and self-respect. When we begin to understand that our talents and abilities (even the ability to earn a lot of money) come not from within ourselves but from God our Creator, we can start slowly letting go of the worldly pride that limits us to only one way of seeing and behaving. Little by little we begin to embrace other thoughts, ideas, and ways of doing things. We expand and bend and begin to focus on God and other people, evaluating all the alternatives available to us.

Consider today's readings. God told Abram He would make of him a great nation. How easy it would have been for Abram to become arrogant, to think, "God chose *me*. I must be better than everyone else." Peter, James and John, who witnessed Christ's Transfiguration, could easily have felt set above other men by what they had seen, the secret they held in their hearts. Even we Christians might be tempted to feel we are set higher than others because Jesus Himself has called us to a holy life.

But as St. Paul wrote, all this is not according to *our* works. What we do and what we have gains us nothing of any lasting value. ***Everything we are comes by God's design and through His grace.*** Only when we embrace God can we find true humility, honor, and self-respect.

This week, let us hand over our "orange" selves to Jesus, and ask Him to help us conquer our worldly, negative pride. As we journey on with Him to Calvary, let us begin to truly listen for and see all the potential ways we might expand and bend in our daily life. Let reach out and embrace all our bothers and sisters, and add their God-given talents and abilities to ours. Let us bring the Light of God into the world in the way God intends us to, not the way we want to. Let us widen our positive, spiritual pride by focusing on God first, so that we may transcend our limitations into the unlimited possibilities that exist in all of God's creation.

Lord, Let Me Walk – Week Two Activities

Rainbow Color: Orange, the color of Pride
Theme of the Week: Transcending Limitations

THOUGHT FOR THE WEEK

"Those who bring Sonshine into the lives of others, cannot keep it from themselves."

(found on a Christian lapel button)

Sunday: How often do you put God's desires for you first? Note one time you did, and one when you didn't. Think about the reasons why you went your own way. How can you begin to change this behavior?

Monday: Do something today you have been putting off, or have left half-done. Finish it.

PROVERBS 21:30 – "There is no wisdom, no understanding, no control, against the Lord."

Tuesday: Reflect on the people who have helped you open yourself —physically, intellectually, and/or spiritually. Write them a note thanking them for their help.

Wednesday: Write down one change you would like to see begin in your life by the end of Lent. Put it where you will see if often, every day. Work on it.

Thursday: Write down a situation in your life that you find hopeless. Find evidence of hopefulness in it. Pray for a change to begin, as God directs.

PROVERBS 16:18 – "Pride goes before disaster, and a haughty spirit before a fall."

Friday: Write down one relationship in which you wear a mask or are afraid to reveal who you are. Begin today to be more honest in that relationship.

Saturday: Share something about your faith that's important to you. Really listen to what the other person says in response. Don't shut it out if it's not what you want to hear. Consider the other person's opinion as you pray for God's guidance.

PROVERBS 12:15 – "The way of the fool seems right in his own eyes, but he who listens to advice is wise."

LORD LET ME WALK

Journeying with Jesus through Lent
The Year of Becoming: Week Three

For this third week of our Journey, our rainbow color is *yellow*, the color of our *intellect*, and our In-Spiraton theme is *Expanding Consciousness.*

The rainbow color yellow is the color of the human mind, which has two parts: intellect and consciousness. Intellect, which is finite, controls our logic center and directs our mental ability to create connections, discover pathways, evaluate facts and make decisions based on what we know. It demands visible proof, scientific explanations and step-by-step directions. Our finite intellect often deceives us into believing that logic is all we need. If we have enough physical facts and arrange them in the proper order, we can ensure both success and happiness.

But we can't. Because human intellect is finite, it sees only the visible and the tangible, and not God, who is Spirit unseen. And only in God can true success and happiness be found.

To see the wondrous things that lie beyond our intelligence, we must use the infinite part of the human mind called consciousness, the part not bound to the flesh. The ability to see the unseen, to expand beyond the finite world into God's infinite domain, resides in our consciousness. Consciousness is part of our soul. In its limitlessness we find no up or down, no north or south, no beginning or ending. Life and love are everlasting and unlimited. God's grace, glory, wisdom and compassion are there for all to see. When we stop relying solely on our flesh-bound intellect and move into our consciousness, we find all the proof we need everywhere we look.

The pathway to expanding our consciousness into infinity is faith; belief and trust in the unseen. When we rely solely on our intellect, we become like the Israelites who saw only the dryness of the desert when they needed water. They could not see beyond their worldly intellect. But if, like Moses, we use faith to guide us and expand our consciousness, God will show us the answers we need and give us the counsel we seek. We will neither doubt nor seek answers in the finite earthly realm, because our expanded consciousness will allow us see into the infinite realm of God.

Always remember, *Jesus knows everything about us*, just as He knew all about the Samaritan woman at the well. His mind is all infinite consciousness. And like the Samaritan woman did, we need to both *listen and see with our expanding consciousness* so that we may share God's message, divine plan, and guidance with others, even if our worldly intellect cannot see any logic in it.

During this third week of Lent, let us focus on turning aside to see God's wondrous kingdom. Spend some time every day with Jesus, even if it's only five minutes, in prayer, reading His word, listening to or singing songs of praise and love, writing in our spiritual journal, having family devotions, etc. Let us ask Him to help strengthen our faith so that the spiritual part of our mind opens wider each day. As our consciousness continues to expand in every direction, let us begin to reflect God's love to the world. And let us extend the hand of God's loving kindness to everyone on earth.

Lord, Let Me Walk – Week Three Activities

Rainbow Color: Yellow, the color of Intellect

Theme of the Week: Expanding Consciousness

THOUGHT FOR THE WEEK

"We are not here to get all we can out of life for ourselves, but to try to make the lives of others happier."

~William Osler

Sunday: Pray Psalm 23 today, and consider how well you truly trust God. How often do your own intellectual abilities keep you from hearing and following God's will?

Monday: Was there a time in your life when you saw beyond the material, into god's infinite kingdom? How did the experience affect you? How did it change your world view?

PROVERBS 14:12 –   "Sometimes a way seems right to a man, but the end of it leads to death!"

Tuesday: Share a story of faith with a friend or relative. Begin to subtly fertilize those around you with God's love.

Wednesday: Gossip rips God's children apart. Spurn it. Today, use words only to build bridges of love and sew seeds of unity.

Thursday: Look carefully at how often you reject people because of their ideas. Don't let this happen today. Listen carefully to everyone, and don't impose your own ideas on them. Expand your mind to accept all views.

PROVERBS 18:2 –   "The fool takes no delight in understanding, but rather in displaying what he thinks."

Friday: Examine your attitude toward money and material things. Just how important are they to you? Are they more important than the spiritual? Could you give them up for God?

Saturday: Be aware of the judgmental statements you make today. Are any based on pride in your own human intellect? Work to stop judging others by their flesh-bound intellectual abilities, or lack thereof.

PROVERBS 27:18 –   "He who tends a fig tree eats its fruit, and he who is attentive to his Master will be enriched."

LORD LET ME WALK

Journeying with Jesus through Lent
The Year of Becoming: Week Four

For the fourth week of our journey our rainbow color is *green*, the color of *Charity and Altruism*, and our In-Spiration theme is *Finding A New And Wonderful World*.

God's New and Wonderful World exists in the domain of Charity and Altruism. In order for us to live there, we must be able to see without judgment and without concern for ourselves.

This means we must move into the realm of Agape. Agape is God's Love, love that has no conditions attached, love that is freely given to everyone and everything no matter what. And to love as God loves, we must be able to see the world as God see it: beautiful, perfect, ideal, and wondrous.

We cannot do that with earthly, human eyes. They see only the physical realm, and tempt us to measure ourselves against the things we call flaws and imperfections. To find a new and wonderful world we must set aside our physical eyes and use our spiritual eyes to see everything as being perfect exactly as it is, because it comes from the hand of God. Only then will our world change. Only then will it become new and full of wonder.

Everything in the world, whether seen or unseen, is connected. It is all One, sprung from the same Source—God. Whatever we do to any one person or thing—including ourselves—we do to everyone and everything. We see it happening daily. Here's just one example: when we abuse our environment, we keep altering the balance of God's ecological system, which in turn affects all living things on the entire planet—plants, animals and people. Worldwide weather patterns change; tornadoes and hurricanes wreak havoc. Internal upheavals cause earthquakes, tsunamis, volcanic eruptions. Poisons in air, water and food cause illness and death. It is all connected.

Consider the lessons from today's readings. In searching for a king among Samuel's sons, God told Jesse not to judge according to physical appearance, but by what is in the heart, the spiritual side of man. Saint Paul told the Ephesians to open their spiritual eyes and live in the Light of Christ, to reject the darkness of looking with physical eyes only. And in John's Gospel, the blind man symbolizes all of us who think we can see though we actually are blind. The clay Jesus put on the blind man's eyes stands for the physical earth on which we daily fasten our own eyes. It is only by washing away the earth that the blind man's eyes are opened, and what he sees is far beyond the physical. So, too, must we wash away the veil that keeps us blind to the glory and wonder of God's world, and open our spiritual eyes to what we can build with God's Love.

This week, let us ask ourselves how wide the band of green Charity is in our own personal rainbow. How often do we judge by appearances instead of what is in a person's heart? How often do we do something without thinking of how our action will impact another living being or our environment? How often do we open our spiritual eyes and see the perfection of God's creation, feast upon the beauty of His Universe, or offer unconditional Agape for everyone we meet?

This week, let us wash away our physical eyes. Let us look for perfection in everything we see, no matter how ugly or flawed by worldly standards. Let us open our spiritual eyes and begin to build God's New and Wonderful World based on true Charity and Devotion to all of Creation.

Lord, Let Me Walk – Week Four Activities

Rainbow Color: Green, the color of Charity
Theme of the Week: Finding A New And Wonderful World

THOUGHT FOR THE WEEK

"We feel and weigh soon enough what we suffer from others: but how much others suffer from us, of this we take no heed."

~Thomas a Kempis

Sunday: Make a list of those people with whom you do not feel at peace. Write or call one of them and reach out a forgiving hand.

Monday: Spend some time with the people in your own family. Show them that you really care about them. Make mealtime a special time for everyone.

PROVERBS 32:3 –   "To do what is right and just is more acceptable to the Lord than sacrifice."

Tuesday: Try to be aware of the effect you have on others today, and pray that you will not be a source of irritation to anyone. If you are, go to that person and apologize.

Wednesday: Write to your representative in Congress, telling how you feel about help for the poor, aid to the hungry, abortion, medical care for the poor and elderly, etc. Encourage your family, friends and neighbors to do likewise.

Thursday: Be aware of how your actions impact the world. Start a strict recycling program at home, and stick with it. Conserve energy. Support an environmental group.

PROVERBS 20:6 – "Many are declared to be men of virtue; but who can find one worthy of trust?"

Friday: Read one unbiased article or book about the people in a place or nation that you consider to be the "enemy." Write down your thoughts as you read. How can you begin to love them?

Saturday: Look into your life to see who you consider a personal enemy. Try to do one positive act toward that person, or toward someone else you do not like.

PROVERBS 16:11 – "Balance and scales belong to the Lord; all the weights used with them are His concern."

LORD LET ME WALK

Journeying with Jesus through Lent
The Year of Becoming: Week Five

Today we mark the fifth week of our Journey with Jesus. Our rainbow color is *blue*, the color of *Spiritual Devotion*. Our In-Spiration theme is *Dormant Talents and Abilities Come Alive*.

True Spiritual Devotion is hearing and obeying the Holy Spirit, the voice of God. In Baptism, the Holy Spirit infuses us with new life, just as in today's readings he instills life in God's people. Throughout our lives He speaks to us, guiding us out of the darkness of the physical world into the realm of Spirit and Light. Our responsibility is to listen to what the Spirit tells us, obey Him, and allow God to use the talents He gave us—both those we are aware of and those we are not—to bring the Light of His Love to the world.

But we must both listen for God's voice *and then obey it*. When Jesus called Lazarus to come forth, Lazarus heard because his physical ears were closed. All he had were spiritual ears. But Lazarus still had a choice. He could have ignored Christ's voice. He had to hear the voice and then obey it in order to find new life. *Hearing without action is meaningless*. It has no value. And if we don't hear, if we are too busy listening to the world, then we have no way to find new life.

We must close our ears to the physical world and open them to the spiritual realm, for it is in Spirit that God speaks to us. And He does so in unexpected ways, not just simply as a voice you hear within you, although sometimes it can be exactly that—a word, phrase or command clearly heard. But His voice can also be the urge to say something nice to a stranger, a nudge to call a certain person, a sudden thought to volunteer our time or expertise. It can masquerade as an opportunity to learn a new skill, sharpen an old one, or use our talent in a new, unplanned way. It can be the offer of a job in an area you'd never before considered or the chance to move to a new location, or come as an invitation to assist, teach, develop, write, sing, direct, cook, sew, dance, design, facilitate, plan, implement, counsel, etc. And when we hear and obey the Spirit, He will always challenge us, stretch us, and move us deeper into Spiritual Devotion and Unity with God.

The more we listen to and obey the voice of Spirit within, the more ways God can use the talents He has given us—often in surprising ways. That's why it's so important to develop our talents to the fullest. We never know when—or how—God will use them. And we must always remember that *all our talents and accomplishments have nothing to do with us*. They come directly from God. We are merely the conduits through which He works. We are His tools. God is in control and He holds the Master Plan. When we listen to Him and obey, we may be surprised by what we accomplish and the paths and opportunities that open up, but God never is.

Let us this week work to widen the blue band of Spiritual Devotion in our rainbow. Let us listen daily to the Spirit within, and obey His call even if we doubt we can do what He asks. We can start in small ways—make that phone call, join that committee—and let God take us where He will. He knows what we are capable of; if we trust in Him, He will bring our Dormant Talents and Abilities alive in miraculous ways as we, through Him, bring the Light of Christ into the world.

Lord, Let Me Walk – Week Five Activities

Rainbow Color: Blue, the color of Spiritual Devotion

Theme of the Week: Dormant Talents and Abilities Come Alive

THOUGHT FOR THE WEEK

"The important thing is this: to be able at any moment to sacrifice what we are, for what we could become."

~Charles du Bos

Sunday: Think of one time when you heard the voice of God guiding your actions. How did you react? Did you obey the summons, or did you question your ability to carry out the command? What was the outcome? Share this memory with someone today.

Monday: When we are praised for our talents it can be difficult to remember they are not really ours, but God's. When you are praised today (or this week, this month, this year), say "thank you" and then verbally give the credit to God.

PROVERBS 16:2 –   "We can always prove that we are right, but is the Lord convinced?"

Tuesday: List the times you find it almost impossible to stop and listen for the Spirit's guidance. What keeps you from listening? What can you do to begin to listen during those times? List them and then put them into practice.

Wednesday: Say yes today if you are asked to volunteer for a committee or to help on a project, especially if you feel you don't "know enough" to be effective. Trust God to stretch you to meet the need. If no one asks, step up and volunteer.

Thursday: Think about how you talk to yourself. Do you sabotage your desire to help by telling yourself you don't know enough or aren't trained enough? What can you do to begin believing you can do it—with God's help?

PROVERBS 20:12 – "If you have good eyesight and good hearing, thank God who gave them to you."

Friday: We are all meant to receive as well as to give. Allow yourself to be on the receiving end of someone's caring today. Being a gracious receiver is a wonderful talent to develop.

Saturday: It's never too late. Think about all the things you've been asked to do, the urges you felt to help out somewhere, the times you desired to learn a new skill—and did nothing about it. Make a list, then pick any one or two and plunge in. See where God will lead you.

PROVERBS 30:5 –   "When a man is trying to please God, God makes even his worst enemies to be at peace with him."

LORD LET ME WALK

Journeying with Jesus through Lent
The Year of Becoming: Week Six

Purple is our final rainbow color, the royal color of *Acceptance*, and our In-Spiration theme is *Being Better Than You Dreamed You Could Be*. As we become more In-Spirited with our Father, His Son, and the Holy Spirit, the purple sliver in our rainbow expands and pulses with awesome majesty, reflecting Christ Himself. God's peace, strength, and joy begin to permeate every fiber of our being.

The more we accept Christ's presence in our lives and walk the road He sets for us on earth, the more we find that our spiritual energy draws people to us. That is the power of this royal rainbow color. The Light of God is irresistible to many. Think of Christ's triumphal entry into Jerusalem. The massed throng of people, drawn to His radiance, celebrated and shouted, Hosanna!" at the sight of Him. So, too, will others be drawn to us. We must always remember that the Light is God's, not ours. We are merely vessels for it. And the nobility of this color does not mean we are better than anyone else, stand higher than others, or are more beloved of God. It simply means that we are better than we used to be. God only compares where we were yesterday to where we are today, for each of us individually. That is the only measurement that matters.

But just as the Light draws some people, it repels others. We may find strangers, friends and even family members turning away from us, for God's Light hurts the eyes of those who are still blind. God's voice wounds ears that are attuned only to physical life. Those who have chosen spiritual darkness and silence will work to undermine our belief and trust in God, so that we take our hand from Jesus' hand and give in to the world's way.

However, as our purple band grows in width, we find it ever easier to turn aside from worldly temptation and endure betrayal. We discover that *God's Light will sustain us* in our sorrow, just as His Light sustained Jesus in His time of travail. Though we may weep for those who betray us, we rest safe in God's loving embrace, knowing nothing can truly harm us.

As we accept the will of our Father for our lives, and live in His presence more and more fully, we find ourselves being lifted beyond the range of our hopes and dreams. Beyond anything we could possibly envision. Beyond, even, our ability to conceive what is it we will become, for our finite minds cannot grasp the glory God has planned for us, the perfect Spiritual union that awaits us in His kingdom. It is a journey both exalting and thoroughly humbling, and at the end we will stand in perfect awe of the person God has made of us through His will and His Agape Love.

This week, let us walk that royal road with Jesus, accepting His presence within us as we radiate His spiritual energy to the world. Let us remember that we are merely vessels for the Light, no better than anyone else on earth. And as we work to be better tomorrow than we are today, let us keep our hand firmly in His when people turn away from us, drawing strength and peace from His presence in our lives. Only by emptying ourselves into God, can we become the person God has always known we truly are. With

God guiding us, Jesus walking beside us, and the Spirit speaking within us, we can move beyond this world into God's kingdom while we are still here on earth. We can become the person God intends for us to be, far better than we could ever dream we would be.

Lord, Let Me Walk – Week Six Activities

Rainbow Color: Violet, the color of Royalty and Acceptance
Theme of the Week: Being Better Than We Dream We Can Be

THOUGHT FOR THE WEEK

"It is better to suffer wrong than to do it, and happier to be sometimes cheated than not to trust."

~Samuel Johnson

Sunday: Take a walk today and meditate on Jesus' entry into Jerusalem. Think about what it must have felt like to be so highly acclaimed and, within a week, so totally rejected.

Monday: Call a relative or friend. Share with them what they really mean to you.

PROVERBS 14:25 –   "The truthful witness saves lives, but he who utters lies is a betrayer."

Tuesday: Ask for and accept forgiveness from someone to whom you have broken a promise. Now, keep the promise— follow through on it.

Wednesday: Call to cheer up someone today, perhaps a somewhat-forgotten older person, or an estranged friend or family member. Begin to repair the bonds of love between you.

Thursday: Think of someone you may have hurt through thoughtlessness, lies or gossip. Call or write, asking for forgiveness. Share Jesus' love with them.

PROVERBS 17:5 – "He who mocks the poor blasphemes his Maker; he who is glad at calamity will not go unpunished."

Friday: Where were you on your faith walk at this time last year? Have you moved forward? If so, how will you continue to grow? If not, what stopped you? Think of at least two ways around the roadblock and put them into action.

Saturday: In every situation today, ask yourself, "What would Jesus do? What would He say? How would He handle this situation?" Try to set aside your own thoughts, feelings and reactions, and listen for God's guidance. Radiate God's presence in everything you do today.

PROVERBS 26:24 – "With his lips an enemy pretends, but in his inmost being he maintains deceit; when he speaks graciously, trust him not."

LORD LET ME WALK
THE JOURNEY'S END – EASTER SUNDAY
The Year of Becoming: Reaching Spiritual Unity

Christ's Lenten Journey has ended. The stone has been rolled away, the tomb found empty. Jesus has conquered physical death and risen into the pure White Light of Life everlasting.

But our journey continues. The process of In-spiration, of Becoming One in Spirit with God, is a life-long journey of self-discovery and personal growth. The six steps of the process— Breaking the Bonds of Emotion, Transcending Limitations, Expanding Consciousness, Finding a New and Wonderful World, Bringing Dormant Talents and Abilities Alive, and Being Better Than You Dreamed You Could Be—lead ultimately to full Spiritual Unity with our Triune God.

Full Spiritual Unity with God. It sounds awesome, daunting, almost impossible. But it's not. Jesus came into the world to make God accessible to everyone on earth—*while they are still alive*. He came not only to show us the way back home, but also how to find and live in His Light while we are here on Earth. Christ's entire life is an illustration of Spiritual Unity, a demonstration of the six steps of In-Spiriting in action. The more balanced our rainbow colors become, the less one color stands out above the others and the more In-Spirited we become. And the more In-Spirited we become, the closer we draw to full Spiritual Unity. Day by day we begin to experience God's purpose, perfection, joy and fulfillment right here on earth. We live in the Light and radiate the Light.

God's Light is the essence of Life. It brings warmth, hope, knowledge, growth, beauty, strength, energy, and confidence. All that has been hidden in darkness is revealed when Light breaks through. What had shriveled and died comes alive again when touched by the Light.

If you bounce White Light through a prism, it breaks into our Lenten colors: red, orange, yellow, green, blue and purple. It is only when these colors are in *perfect balance* that the purity of White Light shines through. So in order to radiate Christ's Light, *our personal rainbow must be in harmony*. If any one color is out of balance, if it's wider than the others, then that is the only color we show to the world. If we are ruled by emotion, we radiate red; if pride owns us, others see only orange. And so on.

Conversely, if any one color is narrower than the rest, the world will never see it in us.

That is why it is vitally important to balance the colors of our personal rainbows. Through Christ's death and resurrection, we have risen with Him into the Light. Think of it: *through Christ, we have actually become human prisms*. And when our colors are in perfect balance, we radiate the pure White Light of the Risen Christ. In perfect balance, we become unified in Spirit with God. In perfect balance, there is no darkness, only pure, white Light.

Life is a series of journeys. The last step of each is merely the first step of the next. Each new event in our lives uncovers obstacles buried deep within that need to be turned over to Jesus: Another color rebalanced; another harmony restored; a closer unity reached.

As we continue daily working the six steps of In-spiration, we grow ever closer to God in Spirit. Our Light shines a little clearer, glows a little brighter. And every day our hearts beat more fully with Love, Humility, and Joy as we radiate God's pure White Light out into the world for all to see and follow.

Lord, Let Me Walk – The Journey Continues
Daily Balancing of Your Rainbow Colors Throughout the Year

THOUGHT FOR THE JOURNEY

"…all we send into the lives of others comes back into our own."

~Mary Kay Ash

MONDAYS: Make Mondays 'stop and think' days. Try to act with love, not react emotionally.

MONDAY PRAYER:

Lord Jesus, help me to act the way You would act in the same situation. Please, Lord, help me balance my rainbow red and Break the Bonds of Emotion.

TUESDAYS: Do things 'someone else's way' on Tuesdays. Stay open to new ways of thinking.

TUESDAY PRAYER:

Lord Jesus, help me not to be arrogant, or to put my way or my ideas first. Please balance my orange color and help me Transcend my Limitations.

WEDNESDAYS: On Wednesdays, listen carefully to what others think and/or suggest. Don't push your own ideas on others. Stay open to the newness and wonder of life.

WEDNESDAY PRAYER:

Lord Jesus, help me use my mind in Your service and to truly listen to and absorb what others say. Balance my yellow and Expand my Consciousness.

THURSDAYS: Dedicate Thursdays to opening your spiritual eyes. See God's perfection everywhere. Think and speak only words of praise, comfort and encouragement.

THURSDAY PRAYER:

Lord Jesus, open my spiritual eyes so that I see Your hand everywhere I look. Expand my green color so that I may find a New and Wonderful World.

FRIDAYS: Make Fridays 'listen for the call' days. Be aware of the voice of Spirit. Say yes to new opportunities and experiences. Give credit to God for your talents and abilities.

FRIDAY PRAYER:

Lord Jesus, open my spiritual ears. Help me hear your call and trust in your judgment. Stretch my blue color as my Dormant Talents and Abilities Come Alive.

SATURDAYS: Make Saturdays 'Sonshine Days.' Share God's Love with everyone in thought, word and deed. Radiate Agape. Let Jesus shine through. Be His conduit.

SATURDAY PRAYER:

Lord Jesus, use me as You need, and help me accept Your will for me. Balance my purple color as you lift me to Become Better Than I Dreamed I Could Ever Be.

SUNDAYS: Explore your growing Spiritual Unity with God. Attend church, read the Bible, meditate, pray, sing, dance—celebrate your relationship with God!

Lord, Let Me Walk

A Journey With Jesus Through Lent

Cycle B:
The Year of Service

BIBLICAL READINGS

LORD, LET ME WALK: CYCLE B
THE YEAR OF SERVICE

Week One Color: Red
Theme: Emotion; Conversion from Sin
Service Action: Feed the Hungry
Readings:
    First: Genesis 9: 8-15
    Second: 1 Peter 3:18-22
    Gospel: Mark 1: 12-15

Week Two Color: Orange
Theme: Pride; Quiet Doubts
Service Action: Clothe the Naked
Readings:
    First: Genesis 22: 1-2, 9a, 10-13, 15-18
    Second: Romans 8: 31b-34
    Gospel: Mark 9: 2-10

Week Three Color: Yellow
Theme: Intellect; Shed Ignorance
Service Action: Shelter the Homeless
Readings:
    First: Exodus 20: 1-17
    Second: 1 Corinthians 1: 22-25
    Gospel: John 3: 13-25

Week Four Color: Green
           Theme: Charity; Comfort Sorrows
           Service Action: Visit the Sick
           Readings:
                First: 2 Chronicles 36: 14-16, 19-23
                Second: Ephesians 2: 4-10
                Gospel: John 3: 14-21

Week Five Color: Blue
           Theme: Spirituality; Patience and Forgiveness
           Service Action: Visit the Imprisoned
           Readings:
                First: Jeremiah 31: 31-34
                Second: Hebrews 5: 7-9
                Gospel: John 12: 20-33

Week Six   Color: Purple
           Theme: Acceptance; Prayer
           Service Action: Pray for the Living and the Dead
           Readings:
                First: Isaiah 50: 4-7
                Second: Philippians 2: 6-11
                Gospel: Mark 14: 1-15 or 15: 1-39

Easter   Color: White
           Theme: Peace; Wisdom
           Service Action: Living in True Servitude
           Readings:
                First: Acts of the Apostles 10: 34a, 37-43
                Second: Colossians 3:1-4
                     Gospel: John 20:1-9

LORD LET ME WALK
Journeying with Jesus through Lent
The Year of Service: Week One

On this, the first week of our Journey with Jesus into Service, our rainbow color is *red,* and our theme is **conversion from sin**. Our weekly Service Action is *Feeding the Hungry*.

Emotions like greed, fear, embarrassment, prejudice and disgust often wreak havoc in our lives. They can drive us to do and say things we normally wouldn't. They can also keep us from doing and saying the things we know we should do or say. Sins of commission or sins of omission—when red rules us, sin becomes the watchword of our lives.

In Genesis this week, we read of the covenant God made with Noah after the flood, a covenant between God and man and every living creature on the earth. That God would make a covenant with us seems reasonable; after all, it was the sin of man that triggered the flood. But animals and birds are not capable of sin. Why would God's covenant be with them, too?

God's inclusiveness underscores the fact that *what we do, and what we fail to do, impacts the entire world* whether we are aware of it or not. Sin doesn't stop with the sinner; it reaches out and eats away at the very fabric of life. When we let our emotions decide our actions, let fear, embarrassment, disgust, hatred, etc., turn us away from what we know is right, we harm every living thing on the earth. Each sin of omission or commission is like a stone tossed in a pond, sending out ripples of pain to every corner of the globe.

Noah had to feed both his family and an ark full of animals and birds for more than a year. This was a physical hunger that needed filling. But feeding the hungry is more than just a physical task. There is also a spiritual component to it, a spiritual hunger that is often more pervasive and debilitating than any physical hunger can ever be. *It is as important to feed people spiritually as it is to feed them physically*. Sometimes it's more important.

Jesus' baptism in the Jordan River bridges the physical cleansing flood of Noah's time and our own spiritual cleansing by the water of Baptism. The forty days and nights that Jesus spent in the desert, resisting the devil's temptations by fasting and praying, illustrate for us the need to connect the physical and spiritual in our lives. *Without the spiritual, we cannot overcome the physical*; they are two sides of the same coin. Hunger, whether spiritual or physical, hardens hearts and keeps people slaves to raw emotion. It builds resentment, fear and hatred, all of which is very fertile ground for sins of omission and commission.

This month, let us work on erasing the emotions that keep us from feeding the physically and spiritually hungry. Let us erase doubt, fear, hatred, embarrassment, anger, disgust. Let us minister in love to our brothers and sisters, give them food for both body and soul. Let us move into full covenant with God as we shrink the red emotion band of our rainbow into perfect balance, so that we, too, may live on God's physical and spiritual food.

NOTE: It's helpful to start a Year of Service Journey With Jesus Journal in which to record your thoughts, prayers, feelings and progress as you Walk With Jesus through Lent. Often, the very act of writing things down makes them more real and a stronger part of our lives. It can also be helpful and enlightening to look back on your journey as the year progresses, and your rainbow continues to grow and shine out to others along their journeys.

Lord, Let Me Walk – Week One Activities

Rainbow Color – Red, the Color of Emotion
Theme of the Week: Conversion from Sin
Service Action: Feeding the Physically and Spiritually Hungry

THOUGHT FOR THE WEEK

"If only we could accept that there is no difference between us where human values are concerned."

~ Liv Ullman

Sunday: Donate food taken from your own cupboard to your local food bank or outreach kitchen. Better still, donate your time along with the food.

Monday: Start an "Emotion Journal." Record the times you said or did something wrong, or didn't say or do what you wanted should have. What were you feeling? What made you act or stopped you from acting? List your emotions and write down ways to deal with those emotions in a positive way.

PROVERBS 10:9 –   "Do not refuse a kindness to anyone who begs it, if it is in your power to perform it."

Tuesday: Cook a meal or dish to share with a poor neighbor, a shut-in, or someone you don't know very well. Tell them they're important to your life.

Wednesday: Give spiritual food to needy souls by really listening to their needs. Give them what they truly need, not what you want them to need.

Thursday: Do something special for someone today, just because they're one of God's children.

PROVERBS 16:3 –   "God does not leave the virtuous man hungry, but he thwarts the greed of the wicked."

Friday: Take a risk and tell someone about God, and His goodness and mercy. Share a time when God's love saw you through a difficulty.

Saturday: Go grocery shopping and leave a full bag or two someone's doorstep. Do this anonymously.

PROVERBS 19:21 –   "A man's conduct may strike him as pure, God, however, weighs the motives."

LORD LET ME WALK
Journeying with Jesus through Lent
The Year of Service: Week Two

Our rainbow color this week is *orange*, the color of *pride and conceit*. Our theme this week is *counseling the doubtful* and our weekly Service Action is *Clothing the Naked*.

Imagine that you are Abraham and God has asked of you the greatest sacrifice anyone could make—to sacrifice your own child. Imagine your anguish, the doubt in your heart, the worldly whispers in your head urging you to deny God's directive. Your emotions (red) surely would rebel against such pain, and your intellect (yellow) question the validity of God's voice. After all, this is your life; only you know what is best for yourself and your family.

This is your orange self responding, the combination of red and yellow that leads to pride and arrogance, the conviction that your mind, your will, are what matters in life.

Abraham, despite whatever doubts and fears he felt, obeyed God. And God stopped his hand, for He does not require living sacrifices from us; Jesus' own death stands as the symbol of our sacrifice. Why, then, do we fear death—and all change is a form of death?

It is the fear of change, of death, of losing our power, our connection to this world, that tends to dictate our lives and actions. The orange part of ourselves, our pride, arrogance, and conceit, clings to what we can see, touch, taste, hear, and smell. This creates the false impression that we have power and control. And pride—in our thoughts and our abilities—gives us the illusion that our will is what matters, that if we run fast enough and accomplish enough, we can control death.

But in our hearts we know the physical is fleeting; *only the spiritual is eternal*. As we learn with Peter, James, and John when they ascended the mountain with Jesus, death is merely a doorway into full spiritual life, a place clothed in Transcendent Light where all dwell in harmony with God. It's a stepping stone into full reality, where the physical has no power or value. Fear and pride kept Peter's words rooted in the world—tents in which physical bodies could shelter. It took darkness to quiet him enough to hear God's words: Listen to Jesus. Listen to God.

Only when we quiet our orange selves, calm the pride that keeps us focused on the physical, can we hear God's will for our lives. When dark times come for ourselves and others, we need to *stop and listen for God's voice*. We need to reach out and calm the fears of others, counsel those who are tormented by doubts, help them learn to hear the voice of God, too. And we need to bridge the physical and spiritual by clothing the naked, those in need both physically and spiritually, with clothing of both cloth and Transcendent Light.

Let us, this week, hand over to Jesus our "orange selves," our need to control what we fear most—change—so that He can bring this rainbow color into balance in our lives. As we journey on with Him to Calvary, let us ask Him to help quiet our minds, to cover us with His soothing darkness, so that we can hear His voice and understand His will for our lives. And let us reach out to others, give solace and counsel to the doubtful, and serve them by providing needed clothing for both their physical and spiritual lives.

Lord, Let Me Walk – Week Two Activities

Rainbow Color – Orange, the Color of Pride and Conceit
Theme of the Week: Counseling the Doubtful
Service Action: Clothing the Physically and Spiritually Naked

THOUGHT FOR THE WEEK

"When the heart weeps for what is lost, the spirit laughs for what it has found."

~Sufi Aphorism

Sunday: In your Faith Journal, list three things in your life that you are dissatisfied with. Pick one and write down ways you can begin to change it, to make it a positive component of your life. Choose the best way and list the steps to make it happen. Do the first step today.

Monday: Clean out your closet and donate all the clothes you haven't worn for a year to an outreach program.

PROVERBS 21:30 –   "There is no wisdom, no understanding, no control, against the Lord."

Tuesday: Reflect on the people who have helped you change— physically, intellectually, spiritually. Write a note or make a call to thank those who have helped you grow in love and grace.

Wednesday: Talk to someone about your spiritual journey. Let that person know how God has taken your life and made positive changes even through the darkest times.

Thursday: Go back through your closet and choose your favorite outfit. Donate it to an outreach program, or to someone who you know could use it.

PROVERBS 5:21 –   "For a man's ways are before the eyes of the Lord, and He ponders all his paths."

Friday: What changes are you most afraid of? Losing a job, downsizing into a smaller house, moving away from your community, your child going out on his or her own? Write it down, then list at least ten ways this change can lead to positive growth for you and your family. Post them where you can see them every day.

Saturday: Volunteer to work at an outreach program, a homeless shelter, a soup kitchen. Bring Light into the lives of others by talking about the impact Jesus has had on your life.

PROVERBS 12:18-19 –   "Lips that tell the truth abide firm forever... the tongue of the wise brings healing."

LORD LET ME WALK
Journeying with Jesus through Lent
The Year of Service: Week Three

For this third week of our Journey with Jesus, our rainbow color is *yellow,* the color of our *intellect.* Our theme is *instructing the ignorant* and our weekly Service Action is *Sheltering the Homeless.*

Hundreds of Jewish laws sprang from God's ten commandments. Rules appeal to our yellow selves; in fact, our minds revel on the challenge of analyzing facts and arranging them into neat, orderly patterns that appear to make sense of the physical world around us. These patterns give us a sense of belonging, a sense of place. When yellow rules, we believe we are in control. Our emotions may balk at the strictures, but our intellect exults in its own connections and conclusions.

But in the New Testament, we find contradictions that put our intellects to the test, anomalies that make us stretch our ideas of what constitutes a home. These contradictions do not have worldly facts as a basic structure. They are founded on spirit, on connections to the life beyond this one, and our yellow intellects have trouble following and believing. When yellow rules, we tend to close our eyes to spirit and turn away from the things of God, from the home He offers us.

God has made it clear that we need the balance of both intellect and faith in our lives to reach into the kingdom of God here on earth. How else can we begin to understand His words about heaven, faith and the Spirit? When the Jews looked for miracles they looked not for the unknown, but for concrete signs from which their intellects could make patterns. The Greeks, in contrast, sought spiritual wisdom without the framework of concrete intellect, and so did not understand the wisdom they found. *Without intellect, one cannot know; without faith, one cannot believe.*

Jesus came to reveal that God's law is based on love, and home is in His arms. His Son came to save us from condemnation by being condemned himself. That enigma is hard for our minds to grasp because there's a spiritual component involved, a faith that we must combine with our intellect. Without it we cannot comprehend infinity on an instinctive level, which is the only level on which we can understand it. When we merge our intellect with faith, God's great love flows over us and we realize that *balance is the way into God's kingdom here on earth*. God's love becomes our home, our shelter and our refuge.

Let us focus this week on giving Jesus our "yellow" minds, so that He can bring us into perfect balance between knowledge and faith. Let us work to find our spiritual home here on earth, the place that is the doorway into eternal life in heaven. And let us use our minds and our hearts to provide both physical and spiritual shelter for our brothers and sisters who walk this earth with us, so that they, too, will not be lost but may have eternal life.

Lord, Let Me Walk – Week Three Activities

Rainbow Color – Yellow, the Color of Intellect
Theme of the Week: Instructing the Ignorant
Service Action: Sheltering Physically and Spiritually Homeless

THOUGHT FOR THE WEEK

"The great lesson is that the sacred is in the ordinary, that it is to be found in one's daily life, in one's neighbors, friends and family, in one's backyard."

~Abraham Maslow

Sunday: Volunteer at a local homeless shelter. Bring God's love with you as you minister to those searching for a home.

Monday: Go without something you really want today. Donate the money to an outreach program to benefit the homeless.

PROVERBS 16: 9 –   "A man's heart plans out his way, but it is God who makes his steps secure."

Tuesday: In your Faith Journal, write about a time when God's embrace felt like coming home. What were the circumstances? What changed as a result of God's love?

Wednesday: Call and volunteer to help instruct children at Sunday school, or in religious instructions classes. Or read the Bible with your children or spouse and talk about what the verses mean to each of you at this moment in your life.

Thursday: What time of day do you feel most at home with God? Make a commitment to spend at least 15 minutes with Him each day at that time. Write down the thoughts and insights you gain each day.

PROVERBS 19:17 –   "The man who is kind to the poor lends to God: the Lord will repay him for what he has done."

Friday: Do you have an extra bed or couch, chairs, tables, rugs, dishes? Do you need all the furnishings you have, or just want them? Donate those items you don't actually need to outreach programs that help furnish places for needy families.

Saturday: How strong is your own Spiritual House? Join a Bible study class to strengthen both your intellectual knowledge and your faith in God.

PROVERBS 3:27 –   "Do not refuse a kindness to anyone who begs it, if it is in your power to perform it."

LORD LET ME WALK
Journeying with Jesus through Lent
The Year of Service: Week Four

Today our Journey takes us to the *green* in our rainbow, the color of *Charity*, of *Love*. Our theme is to *bear wrongs with patience and to forgive injury*. Our weekly Service Action is to *Visit the Sick*.

Disease: the dictionary defines it as illness in general or a particular destructive process in the body. It comes from the prefix 'dis' which means a separation, negation or reversal; and 'ease' which means comfort, freedom from pain or trouble. It is sin on the most basic level: lack of harmony with God and God's Love, both physically and spiritually. When we live in dis-ease, in sin, we turn to the world and to our own devices to solve our problems and end our pain. But the very act of depending only on the world leads to more dis-ease, pain, and hurt.

God's patience with our self-absorbed, worldly ways is shown countless times in the Bible. As we learn today in 2nd Chronicles, He sent messengers time and again to his people, who ignored His word and ridiculed His servants. Even when God made His displeasure known, He still held enough love to allow Cyrus of Persia to rebuild the temple in Jerusalem, so the Jews could find their way back to where God waited in patience for their return.

God's Love is so all-encompassing that He even sent His son to us to act as our surrogate, our Messiah. Totally innocent and pure of Spirit, Christ's blood was shed in substitution for all mankind, so that we would not die an eternal, spiritual death, but rise with Him and live with God through The Lamb, Jesus Christ. This is Love never-ending; it endures all things and forgives all things. Only through God's altruistic Love can we shed the chains of the flesh and heal the dis-ease of body, mind and spirit.

True love does not exist in a vacuum. It reaches out. It sees beyond hurt and deception, penetrates the defenses we erect to protect ourselves from malice and savagery, heals the cruelties we inflict upon each other. It gathers everyone into its gentle embrace, looking past the physical into the spiritual, where we are all one with God.

Perfect Love sees God in everything and everyone, *no matter what*. Jesus never turned away from the sick, the injured, those in physical or spiritual pain. He passed his life among the least fortunate among us, healing with patience and Love. The task He set for us, that He modeled for us, is *to do the same*. Our mission is not turn in fear or disgust from those who suffer illness, but to bring God to them through the love with which we serve them and the grace with which we forgive them.

This week, let us hand over to Jesus our "greenness," so that He can widen this rainbow color in our lives. Let us minister to those sick in body and spirit, gift them with our presence and God's love. Let us work to forgive those who hurt us, whether on purpose or through ignorance. Let us be for them the key to God's pure Love, and lead them—and ourselves—out of dis-ease and back into harmony with Christ Jesus.

Lord, Let Me Walk – Week Four Activities

Rainbow Color – Green, the Color of Charity
Theme of the Week: Forgiving Wrongs and Injuries
Service Action: Visiting the Sick

THOUGHT FOR THE WEEK

"The root of all difficulties is a lack of the sense of the Presence of God."

~Emmett Fox

Sunday: Make a list of those people against whom you bear anger or who you feel injured or betrayed you. Write or call one of them and reach out a forgiving hand.

Monday: Take time to visit a friend or neighbor who is ill in body or spirit. Bring a homemade goodie and spend some time truly listening to this person's feelings and desires.

PROVERBS 32:3 –   "To do what is right and just is more acceptable to the Lord than sacrifice."

Tuesday: Spend the day treating everyone as though they were your best friend. Lend someone a helping hand; listen to someone's problems; buy a homeless person a meal and eat with them. Look for God in everyone you meet today.

Wednesday: Volunteer to visit the sick in the hospital, a nursing home, in your parish. Read an uplifting article or book to them. Share your love of God with them.

Thursday: Think of a time when you felt hurt by someone's actions or words. Did you react with anger, seek revenge? Think of ways to respond with love and list them in your Prayer Journal. Read them often so they stay in your mind for the future.

PROVERBS 29:11 –   "The fool comes out with all his angry feelings, but the wise man subdues and restrains them."

Friday: Look into your life to see who you consider a personal enemy. Try to do one positive act toward that person, or toward someone you do not like.

Saturday: Volunteer to help with a grass roots movement aimed at helping the sick find medical help, the mentally ill receive counseling, to raise funds for research, etc. Look into your heart through prayer to find where your talents can best be used.

PROVERBS 10:12 –   "Hatred provokes disputes, love covers over all offenses."

LORD LET ME WALK
Journeying with Jesus through Lent
The Year of Service: Week Five

This fifth week of our Journey brings us to the color *blue*, the color of *spiritual reverence and devotion to others*. Our theme is *comforting the sorrowful* and our weekly Service Acton is *Visiting the Imprisoned*.

The coming of Jesus marked a rite of passage for us in God's eyes. We ceased being little children in need of hand-holding, close supervision, and instruction in obedience. God's laundry-list of laws no longer reigned supreme; with the Messiah's birth, Love became the only law that mattered. Our spiritual childhood ended with Christ's arrival; for us, Jesus embodies spiritual maturity, and our Father's new covenant, the Covenant of Love, has been written on our hearts. To discover the adult path to God, we need only *be still and listen*.

Obedience is a difficult concept for adults to embrace. We spend our childhood years learning obedience, being punished for transgressions, and waiting for the day when we are old enough to make our own laws. Man's law reigns supreme in our lives. But it is spiritual obedience alone that truly matters, for spiritual obedience is the only way to God. Not until we take our eyes off the world and put them on God will we find the kingdom that waits for us.

How do we obey God's Law of Love? It's easy; He has given us a formula to follow. Our task is to let go of our worldly connections and follow it. It is both the word for what will fill us and an acronym: *JOY*. When we follow the order of the letters, our life will also fall into order: *Jesus*, then *Others*, then *Yourself*. That is the essence of JOY, the sequence to follow to find acceptance and peace in life. Obedience to God's Love is the route that leads us along.

One of the hardest things we can do is to comfort the sorrowing—those who suffer loss, pain, illness, addiction, and imprisonment through negative life choices. Experiencing another's emotional pain makes us feel helpless. We cannot take the burden away, we cannot go back and erase the cause. And deep inside we're afraid for ourselves. It's so easy to turn away from someone imprisoned in sorrow when we don't know what to do or say.

But we don't have to do or say anything. The control belongs to God, not us. We only need to be there, to be present, to lend a comforting arm, a shoulder to cry on, a hot meal, a room cleaned, a laundry load done. *Healing comes from knowing we are loved*. It is enough to be there, to love through your very presence, to trust that God will work through your silence and your touch. It is enough to *love the way God does*, with His whole being. Be still, listen, and He will guide you.

This week, let us ask God to widen our blue selves as we reach out to those in sorrow. Let God love through us as we live in JOY and put others' needs before our own. Let us ask Him to help us seek out those who are imprisoned not only in our correctional facilities, but also those who are imprisoned in their own destructive habits and negative thoughts. Let us learn to Love everyone, especially those who scare us the most, those who we cannot look at without quailing, those we are most afraid to touch. Let us ask God to bring spiritual obedience into our lives and hearts, so that we may find the true path to joy and freedom.

Lord, Let Me Walk – Week Five Activities

Rainbow Color – Blue, the Color of Spiritual Reverence and
Devotion to Others
Theme of the Week: Comforting the Sorrowful
Service Action: Visiting the Imprisoned

THOUGHT FOR THE WEEK

"The important thing is this: to be able at any moment to sacrifice what we
are for what we could become."

~Charles du Bos

Sunday: Visit a shut-in neighbor or parish member.
Encourage them to talk about their life and listen with empathy,
read scripture or uplifting stories to   them, or just sit and be
present with them in loving silence.

Monday: Call your local jail or prison and enquire if there is
someone to whom you could write, someone who doesn't have
family or friends who stay in contact. Write a short letter to that
person asking if they would like to have someone with whom to
share their thoughts and fears.

PROVERBS 114:13 –   "Even in laugher the heart may be sad, and
the end of joy may be sorrow."

Tuesday: Take a risk and share some of your own fears with a friend Let them know that you are grateful for a   listening ear.

Wednesday: Visit a patient in a nursing home. Call ahead and ask if there is someone who doesn't have any visitors. Bring flowers, your Bible or an uplifting magazine like Guideposts or Central Coast Kind and either talk or read to the patient. Make arrangements to come again next week before you leave.

Thursday: Consider how you use words. Do you push confidences away by what you say to people? Do you sound judgmental, or uncaring? Try listening in silence and using body language to convey caring: a pat on the hand or shoulder, a hug, a smile and a nod, etc.

PROVERBS 15:13 –   "A glad heart lights up a face, but by mental anguish the spirit is broken."

Friday: Cook a meal for someone who is in crisis and drop it anonymously at their door.

Saturday: Think about volunteering for Big Brothers or Big Sisters, or a similar organization. Make some calls to find out more information on where you could best use your skills to help others.

PROVERBS 19:20 –   "Listen to counsel and receive instruction, that you may eventually become wise."

LORD LET ME WALK
Journeying with Jesus through Lent
The Year of Service: Week Six

Purple, the color of kingship, is our final rainbow color. It is the color of *majesty and royalty*. Our theme for this week is *praying for the living and the dead*. Our weekly Service Action is to *Bury the Dead*.

Death permeates this week of our journey. Its pall hangs over our heads, dampening our spirits and deadening our hearts. It's hard to see that good can come from such sorrow, hard to comprehend how quickly life can change for what seems the worse. Just as happened to Jesus, we can be riding high one day, be cast down to the depths the next, and experience physical death within another day or two.

Physical life is fragile, yet we live each day with the expectation that it will continue on into the future. But we have no guarantee that will happen. We know, in our heads, that we will die someday. But our hearts refuse to accept that inevitability. Somewhere, deep inside each of us, is the belief that it will never happen to us. It is this belief that keeps us going day-by-day, though all the trials and sorrows we encounter in our physical life. Without the belief that we will prevail and endure, we could not find the strength to persevere and overcome.

That core belief is God's guarantee to His people; *life will never end*, it will go on far beyond anything we can imagine on this earth. The physical will fade away, blown like dust on the winds of time, but our souls will live forever, will dwell in the house of the

Lord, in His glorious presence for all eternity. Our strength to endure the physical trials of life comes from God's presence in our lives. Isaiah tells us that no matter what happens to us, *God's strength is with us always*. And Jesus came to show us how the Father's Love will lift us up beyond the physical into the pure spiritual, into life everlasting. With God on our side, how can anything else prevail?

We tend to close our eyes when faced with the evidence of physical mortality, because we fear our own. Attending wakes and funerals can be extremely difficult. We need always to remember that *God lives within us, works through us, and loves through us*. We are His ambassadors here on earth, and our presence is required for His Love and Compassion to flow freely to those in sorrow. Our presence in the face of death is more than a physical support for the family; it is the spiritual underpinnings of the structure of faith. Our presence confirms that life continues, that God is our strength and refuge.

This week, let us ask Jesus to balance this last color of our rainbow with the others. Let us ask Him to take away our fear of physical death, so that we can bring His presence and comfort to those who are suffering loss. Let us ask for His strength as we attend wakes and funerals and bring God's promise of immortality into the light. And let us ask Jesus to remind us to continue praying for not just the physically living but also the physically dead, to understand that they are living in spiritual bliss with our heavenly Father, waiting for us to join them. This week, let us walk with Jesus into the true life of God's kingdom.

Lord, Let Me Walk – Week Six Activities

Rainbow Color – Purple, the Color of Kingship and Royalty
Theme of the Week: Praying for the Living and the Dead
Service Action: Burying the Dead

THOUGHT FOR THE WEEK

"Death is like a mirror in which the true meaning of life is reflected."
~Sogyul Rinpoche

Sunday: Take a walk today and meditate on the losses you have endured in your life. How did the people who walked through it with you help you understand life and death? Write your insights in your journal.

Monday: Call someone who has lost a loved one and arrange to visit them. Share some of your insights with them.

PROVERBS 14:32 –   "When calamity comes, the wicked are brought down, but even in death the righteous have refuge."

Tuesday: Attend a funeral for someone you have never met. Pray for the soul that has been released into God's Love, and for the family and friends who are sorrowing.

Wednesday: In your journal, write a list of the people, living and dead, who have had the most influence on your spiritual development. Say a prayer for them every day.

Thursday: Write a note to someone you know who has lost a loved one. Let them know you are thinking of them and praying for them. Ask is there is anything you can do, even if it's only a listening ear or ready shoulder.

PROVERBS 19:22 – "What a man desires is unfailing love."

Friday: Think of everyone you know who has died. Imagine them gathered in a room in God's heavenly mansion. Then imagine that you enter that room. What is the first thing they will say to you? Write it in your journal, and your reaction to it.

Saturday: Call or write one living person on the list in your journal. Share your thoughts on God, Jesus, the soul, immortality and the meaning of life.

PROVERBS 26:24 – "In the way of righteousness there is life; along the path is immortality."

LORD LET ME WALK
THE JOURNEY'S END – EASTER SUNDAY
The Year of Service: Living As God's Servant

Christ's Physical Journey has ended. He has risen from the darkness of death into the blazing White Light of the Father. He has become the Servant Blessed, the matrix upon which all life now revolves. And by entering into full Spiritual Life, Jesus enters into each one of us, showing us the way to Love and Serve all humankind.

Hand-in-hand with Jesus, our journey continues. The six steps of Servitude—Feeding the Hungry, Clothing the Naked, Sheltering the Homeless, Visiting the Sick, Visiting the Imprisoned, Praying for the Living and the Dead—when practiced on a daily basis, lead us into a life of true Service with God. They pave the way for us to find true JOY in our lives, and set our priorities where they belong: Jesus first, Others second, Yourself last. For it is only in turning away from the worldly desires of the flesh do we reach our heart's desire: peace, love, and unity with Christ Jesus. We can life a life filled with contentment and inner joy no matter what outside events try to break us down. When we truly walk hand-in-hand with God, nothing can touch or harm us, not even death.

We are sent by God to bring His Light into the world, the pure white light of Love, Compassion and Joy. To do this we must radiate that light in its purest form, all the colors of our own rainbow blended in perfect balance. If we turn away from any one of the steps of unity with God, our rainbow will not balance. We will bring not God's pure light to others, but the unbalanced colors of our own flawed lives. If we let fear rule us, we merely radiate the red of emotion; if pride dominates, we will show only orange to the world.

God's pure white Light brings warmth, hope, knowledge, growth, beauty, strength, energy, and confidence. As God's ambassadors on Earth, we have the duty to radiate this life-affirming Light to everyone, at all times. *God trusts us to help bring His people home to Him*. When we balance our personal rainbows, we become a shining pathway for everyone we meet. We can work in silence, in anonymity; we can volunteer at shelters and food kitchens. We can become active in human rights movements or spend part of each day in prayer. What is important is that we radiate God's Light, each according to the gifts God has bestowed on us. Why? Because *we are the human prisms through which God illuminates the pathway to His heart.*

Life is a series of journeys. The last step of each is merely the first step of the next. Every step along the way interconnects with the others; they cannot be isolated. We cannot choose only those that appeal to us. Each new act of servitude draws us ever closer to God, and brings the whole world one step nearer to full unity. Another color is rebalanced; personal harmony is restored. The world becomes a better place to live, love and flourish.

As we continue daily working the six steps of Servitude, we grow ever closer to God in Spirit. Our Light shines a little clearer, glows a little brighter. God's Light reaches a little farther. And every time we live and act according to JOY, we find a peace that moves us beyond any contentment we can imagine, into the arms of our heavenly Father.

Lord, Let Me Walk – The Journey Continues
Daily Balancing of Your Rainbow Colors Throughout the Year

THOUGHT FOR THE JOURNEY

"If we are facing in the right direction, all we have to do is keep on walking."

~Buddhist Proverb

MONDAYS: Donate food, volunteer at a soup kitchen, or cook a meal for a needy neighbor. Feed spiritual hunger, too, by reading the Bible and talking about God.

MONDAY PRAYER:
Lord Jesus, help me to feed others with both food and Your word. Balance my rainbow red as you teach me to avoid sins of omission and commission.

TUESDAYS: Help organize a clothing drive, work at an outreach shelter or donate an item of clothing you especially like. Encourage family members to clean out their closets, too.

TUESDAY PRAYER:
Lord Jesus, help me not to be selfish when I have more than others. Please balance my orange color as You help me trust in You and quiet my doubts.

WEDNESDAYS: On Wednesdays, go without something and donate the money to the poor. Write in your Spiritual Journal the ways God has given you all you need in life.

WEDNESDAY PRAYER:
Lord Jesus, help me understand that what God gives I am not to keep, but to share. Balance my yellow as I learn more about His word, and His will for me.

THURSDAYS: Dedicate Thursdays to visiting the sick: a friend, neighbor, a nursing home, hospital, Hospice, etc. Work at developing patience, understanding and forgiveness.

THURSDAY PRAYER:
Lord Jesus, open my spiritual eyes to see Your compassion and love. Expand my green color so that I may be a conduit for your saving grace to the world.

FRIDAYS: Volunteer to help bring God's comfort to those imprisoned not only by bars, but also by their own habits, addictions and attitudes. Share from your own heart.

FRIDAY PRAYER:
Lord Jesus, teach me to hold out my hand in comfort and love. Stretch my blue color into balance as I learn to love those less spiritually and emotionally developed than I am.

SATURDAYS: Visit funeral homes and pray for the dead as you bring comfort and solace to even those you do not know. Pray for the deceased, and for those still on this earth.

SATURDAY PRAYER:

Lord Jesus, help me to bring Your love to the bereaved. Balance my purple color as You teach me not to fear death, but to understand its purpose in life.

SUNDAYS: Spend time meditating on the meaning of life, death and unity. Write in your Journal the answers, insights and inspirations with which God gifts you.

Lord, Let Me Walk

A Journey With Jesus Through Lent

Cycle C:
The Year of Transformation

Biblical Readings

Lord, Let Me Walk: Cycle C
The Year of Transformation

Week One	Color:	Red

Theme: Emotion and Seeking
Readings:
    First: Deuteronomy 26:4-10
    Second: Romans 10:8-13
    Gospel: Luke 4:1-13

Week Two   Color: Orange
    Theme: Pride and Transforming Service
    Readings:
        First: Genesis 15:5-12, 17-18
        Second: Philippians 3:17 – 4:1
        Gospel: Luke 9:28b-36

Week Three   Color: Yellow
    Theme: Priorities
    Readings:
        First: Exodus 3:1-8a, 13-15
        Second: 1 Corinthians 10: 1-6, 10-12
        Gospel: Luke 13: 1-9

Week Four   Color: Green

              Theme: Altruism, Charity and Forgiveness

              Readings:

                   First: Joshua 5: 9a, 10-12

                   Second: 2 Corinthians 5: 17-21

                   Gospel: Luke 15: 1-3, 11-32

Week Five   Color: Blue

              Theme: Obedience Through Loss

              Readings:

                   First: Isaiah 43: 16-21

                   Second: Philippians 3: 8-14

                   Gospel: John 8: 1-11

Week Six   Color: Purple

              Theme: Acceptance and Trust

              Readings:

                   First: Isaiah 50: 4-7

                   Second: Philippians 2: 6-11

                   Gospel: Luke 19: 28-40 and 22:14-23:56

Easter   Color: White

              Theme: Harmony and Balance

              Readings:

                   First: Acts of the Apostles 10:34a, 37-43

                   Second: Colossians 3:1-4

                   Gospel: John 20:1-9

LORD LET ME WALK

Journeying with Jesus through Lent
The Year of Transformation: Week One

This week, the first week of our Journey With Jesus into Transformation, our rainbow color is *red*, and our Transformation theme is *emotion and seeking*, learning to trust in God's power and faithfulness to transform our lives.

The word emotion comes from two Latin words: 'e', meaning 'out'; and 'movere', meaning 'to move'. It is a word that we use as a noun to define what we feel, but in reality it actually describes *an action*—to move out into a red state, a state where only emotion exists.

Often, when we experience strong feelings like love, hope, joy, curiosity, hate, fear, anger, frustration, or despair, it seems as though we move out of ourselves into a state where logic and cool headedness have no place. We react without thinking about the consequences. We give in to the temptations surrounding us even though we know it is wrong. When we react in this state, we usually are either sorry for what we said or did, or we are relieved that no harm was caused. Often people describe the sensation of "moving out" in such ways: I had no control; Something came over me; I saw red and I couldn't think, I just acted; I felt like I had been split in two and I couldn't stop the other me. Haven't we all felt like this at one time or another?

Loss of control over our words and deeds can be frightening, and scary enough to make us deny our emotions, to bury what we feel. But *feelings are a normal part of who we are*. They cannot be denied or shut off without causing us irreparable damage. It is important for us to understand that feelings are neither right nor wrong. They just are. They exist outside of judgment. *It is what we do, how we act when we deal with our feelings, that determines right or wrong*. It is our attachment to worldly things that makes and keeps our emotions so strong. Only when we care so much about something do we feel that deeply about it, whether it be the things we own, our opinions, our dreams and ideas, our reputation or our career.

Feelings act as signposts that highlight the choices along our life path. Too often we blindly go in the direction we think they point toward. We move out into our 'red selves' and let emotion take control. But if we follow the example Jesus set for us, we can use our emotions the way they are meant to be used, as a way to better understand ourselves and our attachment to the world, and to come closer to God.

Consider how Jesus dealt with temptation after spending 40 days and nights fasting and praying in the desert. Weak and hungry, He was offered food, riches, power, and glory by the devil. We can only imagine the human emotions He felt: hunger and thirst, surely, but also perhaps resentment, anger, indignation, dejection, jealousy, melancholy, desire and envy. But He did not give in to temptation; He did not move out of Himself into the emotions of the moment. He knew that the Path is not part of this world. The Path leads *through* the world *to* God. Gently but firmly He held strong in the face of His human feelings.

The strength of our emotions show us how attached we are to the things of this world. But as Jesus said, "Man does not live by bread alone." The secret to handling our emotions is to trust God, to attach ourselves to God, for then our emotions lose power over us.

This week, let us give Jesus our human emotions, that He may help us deal with them, and begin to detach us from our worldly possessiveness. Let us keep our hand in His as we deal with the many temptations that come our way in our daily lives, and learn to trust in God's power and faithfulness. And let us ask Jesus to help shrink the red emotion band of our rainbow into perfect balance, so that we, too, may not live by worldly bread alone.

NOTE: If you haven't yet, you may want to start a Year of Transformation Journey With Jesus Journal in which to record your thoughts, prayers, feelings and progress as you Walk With Jesus through Lent. Often, the very act of writing things down makes them more real and a stronger part of our lives. It can also be helpful and enlightening to look back on your journey as the year progresses, and your rainbow continues to grow and shine out to others along their journeys.

Lord, Let Me Walk – Week One Activities

Rainbow Color: Red, the Color of Emotion
Theme of the Week: Seeking, Trusting in God's Power and Faithfulness

THOUGHT FOR THE WEEK

"The strength of a person consists in finding out the way in which God is going, and going that way, too."
~Henry Ward Beecher

Sunday: Look at one value in your life that you preach better than you live. Start today to live it better as each day passes.

Monday: Look for the good in everyone you encounter today. (This may not be as easy as you think!)

PROVERBS 3:5 –   "Trust in the Lord with all your heart and lean not on your own understanding."

Tuesday: Examine whether you accept people as they really are. Are you overly critical of them? Examine any strong negative feelings you may have. Where do they come from? Why do you feel that way? Be honest, then give those feelings over to God.

Wednesday: Tell someone about one part of your life you are trying to change. Ask them to help you become a better person in that area.

Thursday: Pray for gentleness. Do something special for someone. Give them what they really need, not what you want them to need.

PROVERBS 1:7 –   "The fear of the Lord is the beginning of knowledge, but fools despise wisdom and instruction."

Friday: Pray to be open to those with whom you do not agree. Do not argue with anyone today. Let go of anger for just one day.

Saturday: Try to be aware of the needs of others. Recognize whose needs you place first –yours or others'. One time today, consciously put someone else's needs first.

PROVERBS 4:23 –   "Above all else, guard your heart, from everything you do flows from it."

LORD LET ME WALK

A Journey with Jesus through Lent

The Year of Transformation: Week Two

This week our rainbow color is *orange*, and our transformation theme is *pride and service*, service that will bring about a transformation in our lives.

Who among us has not experienced that warm flush of pride when something we have done or said is acknowledged for its importance or greatness? It's a wonderful feeling, one that tells us we are special, perhaps better than others. And it is a feeling that is very easy to become addicted to.

This is especially so because the world in which we live values excellence above all else, and pits one person against another in contest after contest. Those who "do better" than the rest are rewarded with marvelous honors: scholarships, testimonials, trophies and medals, bonuses, awards, promotions, even fame and fortune. Winning is everything; if you aren't the best, you're worthless.

This world view feeds directly into our "orangeness"—the color of ambition, of pride in our intellect and abilities. A combination of emotion and intellect, this "orange" part of us keeps us striving for the worldly goals we have set for ourselves. It keeps us stubborn and stiff, unable to bend and change, incapable of hearing when God asks us to let go, or tells us to alter our direction. Like Peter on the mountain, who wanted to take charge and arrange things to his own liking, we forge ahead with our own plans when we need to stop, listen to Jesus, and re-evaluate our lives.

Consider this week how Abram sat in silence waiting for God's answer, even in a deep and terrifying darkness (perhaps that of his own "orange self"?). He did not rush out to conquer the lands promised him; he did not rely on his own desire, power or intellect. He waited in unquestioning obedience and servitude, and in God's time was rewarded.

We are to be like Abram; not the master who charts the destiny, but the servant who listens and serves in love as his Master wishes, always ready and always obedient to the Master's way. And, as we learn in a blaze of light on another mountain with Peter, James and John, it is Jesus—our Father's beloved Son—who is the Master to whom we are to listen, the Light we are to follow and serve in a world full of the darkness of our own pride and ambition.

Let us, this week, hand over to Jesus our "orange selves", our need to be on top—to be master, controller, decision-maker. Let us begin to live in silence, rather than tooting our own horn for the world to admire and honor. And as we journey on with Him to Calvary, let Him be the Master, let Him control the means and decide our way for us. Let us listen to Him, and begin to integrate into our lives the goals He sets for us. And let us let go of the overabundance of "orange" that keeps us in the dark as we transform ourselves by moving out into the Light of love and service.

Lord, Let Me Walk – Week Two

Rainbow Color: Orange, the color of Pride
Theme of the Week: Service and Transformation

THOUGHT FOR THE WEEK

"Transformation in the world happens when people are healed and start investing in other people."
~Michael W. Smith

Sunday: Write down three characteristics that mark your relationship with God. Consider what you can do to change those you are dissatisfied with, and strengthen the rest.

Monday: Stop procrastinating. Look at what you have not finished and keep working on it until it is done.

PROVERBS 30:5 –   "Every word of God is flawless; He is a shield to those who take refuge in Him."

Tuesday: Reflect on the people who have helped you change—physically, intellectually, spiritually. Thank those who have helped you grow in love and grace.

Wednesday: Write down one change you would like to see begin in your life by the end of Lent. List the steps you need to take to accomplish this change, then mark off each step as you do it.

Thursday: Pray that God will give you the direction you need to find hope in a situation that you feel is hopeless. Try to think more like God does, to look for the hope you can find if you allow God to work through you.

PROVERBS 27:17 –   "As iron sharpens iron, so one person sharpens another."

Friday: Write down one relationship in which you wear a mask or are afraid to reveal who you are. List out ways you can begin to be more honest about who you truly are, then follow them, one by one.

Saturday: Talk to someone about your faith today. Tell them about God and what He has done for you in your life. Invite that person to come to church with you.

PROVERBS 12:15 –   "The way of the fool seems right in his own eyes, but he who listens to advice is wise."

LORD LET ME WALK
A Journey with Jesus through Lent
The Year of Transformation: Week Three

For this third week of our Journey, our rainbow color is *yellow* and our transformation theme is *priorities*.

Yellow is the color of the intellect, the human mind. The yellow in our rainbow controls our logic center and directs our mental ability to create connections, discover pathways, evaluate facts and make decisions. It is the color of mathematics and science, the part of us that demands visible proofs, scientific explanations and step-by-step directions—even for the things of God. But God and His ways are not comprehensible to flesh-bound intellects such as ours. Our minds cannot grasp infinity. And so we rarely turn aside from worldly concerns to see the wondrous things beyond our intelligence.

A highly functioning mind is coveted in our society; we have even devised tests to measure a person's Intelligence Quotient (IQ), and hand out awards for intellectual excellence. It is all too easy to consider those with high-functioning minds as being better than the rest of humanity; indeed, scientists and mathematicians hold an honored place in our world.

But God makes it clear in today's readings that we are all equal in His sight. He nourishes us all in the same way; how we accept and use God's spiritual nourishment is what counts, not how well-developed our intellectual abilities are. In fact, intellectual ability can sometimes interfere with our spiritual side, for God is not knowable in human terms. Intellectual capacity only measures smartness in relation to the world, not in relation to God.

It can be very difficult not to place too much emphasis on intelligence when we live in a world that stresses its importance. And it can be almost impossible to let go of our dependence on our ability to assess facts and make logical decisions, and bow to the will of God, which can often feel illogical in human terms. But in the parable of the fig tree, Jesus asks us not to be the person who plants the tree and decides its fate—the person who uses intellect alone to make decisions—but to be the gardener who nourishes the tree with love and coaxes it to bear fruit with which to nourish others. We are to place top priority on living as God needs us to live, serving and nourishing his people in spiritual, not intellectual, ways. If we keep God and His ways first in our lives, all else will follow in His orderly fashion, even if our "yellow selves" cannot see any worldly logic in it.

Let us focus this week on doing everything as God would have us do it—for Him and His Glory—not as our minds tell us we should do it. Let us turn aside to see His wondrous things. Spend some time every day with Jesus, even if it's only five minutes, in prayer, reading His word, listening to or singing songs of praise and love, writing in your spiritual journal, having family devotions, etc. And let us give Jesus our "yellow" minds, that He may curtail our dependence on our own intellect, and set our priorities firmly with God first, others second, and then ourselves. Let us transform into the gardeners of humanity, cultivating and fertilizing others so that they, too, may grow the nourishing fruit of God.

Lord, Let Me Walk – Week Three Activities

Rainbow Color: Yellow, the color of Intellect
Theme of the Week: Priorities

THOUGHT FOR THE WEEK

"Life is a moving, breathing thing. We have to be willing to constantly evolve. Perfection is constant transformation."

~Nia Peeples

Sunday: Pray Psalm 23 today, and consider how well you truly trust God. How can you begin to turn over your anxieties and worries to God? What do you need to change in order to truly live in God's word?

Monday: Go without something you really want today. Donate the money anonymously to a charitable cause.

PROVERBS 29:18 –   "Where there is not revelation, people cast off restraint; but blessed are those who heed wisdom's instruction."

Tuesday: Share how God has begun to transform you with a friend or relative. Fertilize those around you with God's love.

Wednesday: Don't let an angry or belittling word cross your lips today. Let everything you say work to build bridges of love and sow seeds of unity.

Thursday: Carefully consider everything you hear, and don't reject ideas just because you don't agree with them. Instead, discuss how agreement can be reached between you and others, how you ideas might meld together into a new whole that serves everyone.

PROVERBS 18:2 –   "The fool takes no delight in understanding, but rather in displaying what he thinks."

Friday: How important are money and possessions to you? Give up coffee, cigarettes, chocolate or some other addictive luxury today, and trust that God will fill the void with His peace and love.

Saturday: Be aware of how often you judge other people and ideas. What makes you need to judge others instead of accepting them? Work to change that aspect of yourself.

PROVERBS 9:10 –   "The fear of the Lord is the beginning of wisdom, and knowledge of the Holy One is understanding."

LORD LET ME WALK

A Journey with Jesus through Lent
The Year of Transformation: Week Four

ALTRUISM: Generosity – magnanimity – heroism – self-denial – devotion – unselfish – chivalrous – putting oneself in the place of others.

CHARITY: Benevolence – good-will – loving kindness – obliging – humane – forgiving – God's love – God's grace – entering into the feelings of others.

Blue is the color of the fourth week of our journey, and our transformation theme is *altruism, charity and forgiveness*.

Today our Journey takes us into more difficult territory, for it requires of us a sacrifice of heroic proportions. As Saint Paul writes to the Corinthians, Jesus took on our burden of sin. He actually became sin, cutting Himself off from communion with His Father and dying in sacrificial substitution for us, so that we could be reconciled to God the Father. We have been forgiven, and have been entrusted to bring the message of reconciliation to the world.

This is altruism—devotion to the interests of others without regard to self—at its most supreme, most perfect. For what did Jesus have to gain by this sacrifice? He is God; perfect, spotless, totally innocent, incapable of sin, dwelling eternally in Heaven with His Father. He has no need of cleansing. He has no need of forgiveness. He has absolutely nothing to gain. But so great is His capacity to actually participate in our feelings and ideas, that in His perfect mercy He chose to put our interests first, to transform Himself to become the vileness of sin itself, so that in His death we can find our way out of sin into eternal life.

Here is the example set for us: the green of altruism, merciful love and empathy, as perfected in God's own Son, Jesus, and as illustrated in the Parable of the Prodigal Son. This son had done nothing to deserve his father's forgiveness; indeed, he had done almost everything to drive his father away! Without earning it, he had taken his share of the estate his father had worked hard to acquire, and then squandered it. He had lived, even reveled, in sin: gluttony, avarice, adultery, gambling—everything an honest, hardworking person reviles. And when it was all gone, he came home.

From our human standpoint, that father would have been justified in turning this young man away from his house, in writing him off because of the hurt and betrayal he had caused. But he didn't. He was overjoyed that his lost son had returned. In the spirit of true, unconditional love, the same Agape Love our heavenly Father has for us, this father opened his arms, welcomed his son and celebrated his return. This is the Love we are to show to each and every person we meet.

This week, let us ask ourselves how wide the band of green is in our own personal rainbow. We all feel empathy tugging at our heartstrings, especially when those we love, those we are closest to, are hurting, either physically or emotionally. Many times we would gladly take the burden on ourselves, if we could, to ease their pain, especially if it is a family member. But how many of us can honestly say we would do the same for a casual acquaintance, a perfect stranger, or an enemy—those whom we truly dislike, those who have hurt us beyond our human capacity to forgive?

We must remember that in transforming Himself to become human, Jesus died for all of us—even for those who spat on Him, mocked Him, beat Him, crushed thorns on His head and pounded nails into His hands and feet. He put no conditions on His sacrifice and left no one out, neither friend nor enemy.

So, too, must we transform our "green selves," widen ourselves to include our enemies. Jesus told us to love one another—not just our family and friends, not just our fellow parishioners, but everyone everywhere, no matter who they may be: the drunk driver who injures or kills someone we love; the mechanic who is dishonest and defrauds us; the once-friend who spreads vile gossip about us; the thief who steals from us; the son or daughter who defies us; the husband or wife who ignores or cheats on us; the person so consumed by anger that he flies airplanes into buildings. Love each and every one, no matter how hard it is.

This week, let us hand over to Jesus our "greenness," so that He can widen this color in our lives. Let him lead us gently into empathy and love for all of the people we meet each day. Let us not judge, for judgment is God's domain. Our domain is to love, to "walk a mile in their shoes," to learn to understand and empathize with those around us. To learn not to love, but to Love.

Let us ask Jesus to teach us this week how to do these things: how to put others first; how to see and understand what another person feels; and how to transform ourselves in Love to serve them —to die, in our own small way, so that others can feel God's Love pouring through us—perhaps for the very first time in their lives.

As Jesus became for us the key to eternal life, let us this week expand our "green selves" to become for others the transformative key to Jesus and His Love.

Lord, Let Me Walk – Week Four Activities

Rainbow Color: Green, the color of Love
Theme of the Week: Charity, Altruism and Forgiveness

THOUGHT FOR THE WEEK

"The purpose of meditation is personal transformation."

~Henepola Gunaratana

Sunday: Make a list of those people who bother you for one reason or another. What are the feelings you have inside about those people? List ways you can begin to change those feelings.

Monday: Let one person in your family know the "real you," the person you hide from the world. Let that person know your failings and your fears. Discuss ways can change your fear of not being "good enough."

PROVERBS 17:22 –   "A cheerful heart is good medicine, but a crushed spirit dries up the bones."

Tuesday: Everything we do has an effect on others. Work today to make sure your effect will be positive and encouraging to everyone you meet.

Wednesday: Look for one area of social justice where you can become involved: help for the poor, aid to the hungry, abortion, medical care for the poor and elderly, etc. Volunteer at meetings, talk to friends and family about the issue, spotlight it on social media. Don't sit on the sidelines anymore, on that one issue.

Thursday: Let yourself be inconvenienced at least once this day. Sacrifice you time to lend a hand. Love the person who needs your help.

PROVERBS 16:3 –   "Commit to the Lord whatever you do, and He will establish your plans."

Friday: In our media-influenced society, it's easy to consider those from another nation as "the enemy." Today, read a book about the people from that country, or try to meet someone from that country. Look carefully to find areas of commonality between you. Begin to change that "enemy" into a friend.

Saturday: Look into your life to see who you consider a personal enemy, someone who has not treated you well. Today, do one nice thing for that person, or say something nice about him or her to others.

PROVERBS 16:9 –   "In their hearts human beings plan their course, but the Lord establishes their steps."

LORD LET ME WALK
A Journey with Jesus through Lent
The Year of Transformation: Week Five

This fifth week of our Journey finds us nearing the end as, with Jesus, we encounter a woman guilty of adultery and, through Him, learn to bow our will to our Father's. The lessons are getting harder, hitting closer to home, with blows that can feel shattering to human egos. Our rainbow color this week is *blue*, the color of *religious or spiritual devotion and veneration*. Our transformation theme is *learning obedience through perseverance and loss*, to participate fully in reconciliation with God.

Blue corresponds to that piece of us which expresses our spiritual or religious reverence, and our devotion to the interests of others. The width of this color in our personal rainbow measures the depth of our relationship, through Jesus, with the Triune God Himself, in His capacity as Father, Mentor, Teacher, Leader and Pilot of our lives. It is the yardstick by which God judges our attachment to the physical world around us, the importance we place upon our material life over our spiritual life. It is, in a way, the color of eternity.

Eternal salvation is open to all of us through Jesus, who walked this earth as a human man, and learned obedience through suffering, loss and tears. When this obedience was perfected in His sacrificial death as atonement for our sins, Jesus became, for all who obey Him, the source of salvation for everyone on earth. It is through our own suffering that we become perfected within our own human bonds, and become a pathway to Jesus for others around us. It is only when we stop fighting and questioning, and become able and willing to bend totally to God's will in our lives, that we find the yoke we fought against is, indeed, sweet.

But it is one thing to say that the Lord works all things to good for those that love Him, and quite another experience suffering in our own lives. It's so hard to watch a loved one battling cancer or crippling disease. It's even harder to cope with sudden death. It's agonizing to see your children lured down the path of drug or alcohol abuse; to witness your possessions lost through fire, earthquake, storm or other accident; to discover the faithlessness of a marriage partner or close friend; to be the victim of a scam that empties all your bank accounts.

How can our human minds possibly comprehend how God can use such things to help transform us, much less for the greater glory of mankind? How can our pain, tears and bewilderment possibly benefit even ourselves, much less our fellow men?

It seems impossible, but God does take the bewildering, the confusing, the painful, frightening and tragic events of our lives, and uses them to make us see ourselves as we truly are. He requires that we look ourselves straight in the eye and acknowledge our faults and shortcomings. He requires that we accept there are things in this world that touch our lives intimately that we cannot control, change, stop or affect in any way. *There are problems and trials through which we cannot make it alone.*

Consider the woman who was caught committing adultery. Old Testament law decreed she be stoned to death for her sin. She had no control over her fate; she had lost everything: her home, her possessions, her family, even her life. She did not struggle against this fate. She had already accepted what was to happen, and stood quiet as a strange man, one she thought a simple Teacher, pronounced her doom. But when Jesus told the crowd, "Let the one among you who is without sin be the first to throw a stone at her," the crowd dispersed, and He gave the woman her life back by refusing to condemn her too.

In this He teaches us that when we detach from the world, our losses, though seen as tragedies by human standards, will stand as a triumph of true forgiveness, love and life that will radiate out to the world. God is in control and He holds the Master Plan. We are never, ever alone; things will always work out for His Glory.

But we only receive that knowledge and strength when we let this world totally go and turn full control over to Him; when we transform ourselves. God gifts each of us with a free will. He allows each of us our own choices in life, and He will not interfere with our decisions.

We can choose to rant and rave, to question, "Why? Why me? Why this? Why won't You make it stop?" We can let our hearts and our lives be swallowed in bitterness and hatred; we can judge all around us as though we were without sin ourselves. Or we can let go and accept, for it is only when we fully turn back over to Him control of His material creation that His peace descends upon us, His knowledge enfolds us, and His strength sustains us. When we let go, God can work miracles in our lives for the good of all humankind.

This week, let us ask Jesus to widen this eternal blue color in our rainbow. Let us ask Him to help us through the emptiness and grief, the helpless and hopeless times in our lives, the confusing and degrading experiences, the humiliation and isolation we all feel at times. Let us ask him to help us let go of our worldly attachments and lead us into true acceptance of our Father's will.

If through the pain we can remember to grasp the comforting hand that Jesus holds out to us, we can transform our seething fury and galling bitterness into humble devotion to God. We can convert the bewilderment and the questioning that attack us into total acquiescence to His will and loving adoration of His daily presence in our hearts.

In doing this, we give God free rein to turn our personal tragedies into miraculous triumphs for the glory of His name, that all might see and come to believe in Jesus, the Lord. Through our suffering and loss we can become, for others, the pathway to Jesus, who is the gateway to eternal salvation. Can there be any greater purpose for our life?

Lord, Let Me Walk – Week Five Activities
Rainbow Color: Blue, the color of Spiritual Devotion
Theme of the Week: Learning Obedience through Suffering and Loss

THOUGHT FOR THE WEEK

"When someone chooses to value herself over the things she can buy, true transformation begins."

~Suze Orman

Sunday: Remember one time when your faith in God helped you over a difficult time. What did you learn from it? How did it make you stronger, closer to God? Share that event and your conclusions with family members, a friend or a casual acquaintance.

Monday: Sometimes it is much harder to accept forgiveness than it is to give it. (It's hard to admit when we've been wrong!) Pray that you will be able to graciously and gratefully accept the forgiveness of others, as well as of God.

PROVERBS 3:6 – "In all your ways submit to Him, and He will make your paths straight."

Tuesday: List the blind spots you find in your own life. What can you do to see more clearly from now on? Apologize to someone in your family or to a friend who you may have hurt because of your blindness.

Wednesday: Make today "visiting day." It doesn't matter if it's a friend, a relative, or even a stranger. Visit someone in a nursing home, or a sick friend or relative. Bring them something special to show your caring and love.

Thursday: Consider how you use your words. Are there people you have hurt by your words? What can you do about it? Say something kind to everyone you meet today.

PROVERBS 15:16 –   "Better a little with fear of the Lord, than great wealth with turmoil."

Friday: Receiving is a gift we offer to others when we accept their help and caring. It's as important a gift as is giving, because it allows others to show their own growing altruism. Allow yourself to be on the receiving end of someone's caring today.

Saturday: Take a few of your favorite canned goods from your cupboards to Operation Good Neighbor, or donate them to your local Food Pantry. Clean out your closets and donate some of your favorite clothes (not just the things that don't fit anymore) to your local thrift store.

PROVERBS 21:1 –   "Whoever loves discipline loves knowledge, but whoever hates correction is stupid."

LORD LET ME WALK
A Journey with Jesus through Lent
The Year of Transformation: Week Six

Purple is our final rainbow color, the color of majesty and royalty, the color of kingship. Our transformation theme is *acceptance of and trust in God's will.* As Jesus becomes a larger and ever-present force in our daily lives, the tiny purple sliver on the bottom of our rainbow selves brightens, expands and pulses with awesome majesty reflected from Christ Himself. As our union with our Father, His Son and the Holy Spirit becomes more complete, the rainbow of our self becomes balanced within Jesus' loving hands. God's peace, strength and joy permeates every fiber of our being. This royal mantle spreads over us for all the world to see, a captivating signpost for others on their Journeys to and with Jesus.

Imagine Jesus in a quiet moonlit garden just a few days after his triumphal entry into Jerusalem. It is late at night; time is running out. He has come to human acceptance of His Father's will. He knows He will never see another sunset. He is physically exhausted, emotionally drained—and the ordeal before Him has not even begun! But spiritually He is at His strongest, upheld through prayer by unswerving trust God's power and love.

Then He rises, turns, and sees a man who has spent three years at His side, working, traveling, breaking bread, sharing the good and bad times, listening to His preaching, watching miracles unfold. Judas, His friend, His disciple. Imagine Jesus' pain as, with a kiss—the universal sign of love and friendship—He is betrayed by His friend into the hands of His enemies.

Even though Judas spent those years with Jesus, listening, sharing and observing, he had not opened himself to God nor grown in trust or love. Enslaved by his own pride, greed and fear, caught between the powers of darkness and the Power of Light, he had to choose. He chose darkness, and Jesus died.

So it is for all of us. We cannot stand neutral. We must choose. And as those of us who choose God draw ever closer to Him, as Jesus' living hands balance our rainbow colors, those who have chosen darkness are repelled by the Light of God's awesome presence in our lives. It hurts their eyes, points up their faults and shortcomings, reveals the ugliness in their lives and exposes the falseness of the world system upon which their existence is based. And so they will betray us in many different ways, undermining our foundations of belief and trust in God, making the road so rocky and fear-filled that we will take our hand from Jesus' hand and give in to the easy way—the world's way.

It is the hidden duplicity in Judas' loving embrace and kiss that shows the subtle forms these attacks on our faith can take. We find them in movies, television, newspapers, books, advertising, stories and magazine articles, all of which preach 'me first,' 'pleasure above all,' and greed, gain and envy. They teach us to act, speak and dress according to worldly whims. Every day we find God rarely acknowledged; human secularism litters our children's schoolbooks; peer, social and corporate pressures increase daily; legal injustice is rampant. We are bombarded in a score of hidden ways, day by day.

But most hurtfully, we too are beaten and bruised by friends who turn on us as we walk closer to God, doing His work. They will use open slander, gossip and lies to discredit us and turn others against us, or simply be content with nasty looks, a turned back, or a cold shoulder.

It seems incomprehensible that, in the twenty-first century, our growing closeness with God can trigger such behavior. But God's presence in our lives makes us not only daily witnesses to the world, but also targets for Satan's minions. We must be prepared to stand firm in the strength of our Father, in our trust in His power, to suffer such persecutions for Jesus' sake, to uphold the Spirit and faith that fills us. We must remember, even in our pain, that God has purpose and direction in these persecutions. When we stand firm stand in God's righteousness we help others find the way to Jesus. Though it hurts greatly to lose friends—or even family members—in this way, we must remember that people always come and go in our lives. But Christ's Love, which sustains and strengthens, will remain with us throughout eternity.

This week, let us hand over to Jesus this last color of our rainbow, so that He can balance it with the rest. We know that He, too, suffered the wrenching agony of love turned sour, and friendship lost through fear or hatred. Let us ask Him to help us stand firm in His principles, strong in our faith, and joyful in His love, wearing our royal purple mantle for all to see. Let us keep our eyes on Him when we suffer for His sake at our friends', or the world's, hands, knowing God will use our pain to transform out lives for the benefit of His children.

Most of all, let us ask Jesus to wipe away any anger and bitterness we feel toward those who betray us and our love, for they really unknowingly are betraying God Himself. Let us this week, and for all our lives, pray sincerely that Jesus will replace our anger and bitterness with His infinite capacity for compassion and love.

"Father, forgive them; they know not what they are doing."

Lord, Let Me Walk – Week Six Activities
Rainbow Color: Violet, the color of Royalty, Kingship
Theme of the Week: Acceptance and Trust

THOUGHT FOR THE WEEK

"I think that any time of great pain is a time of transformation, a fertile time to plant new seeds."

~Debbie Ford

Sunday: Spend some time alone today to think about what Jesus went through, first being highly acclaimed and, within a week, totally rejected. How do you deal with betrayal? Try to list ways you can understand what the betrayer is feeling, and send that person your love and caring despite the hurt.

Monday: Open yourself up enough to share with one person what they mean to you, how important they are in your life. Understand that your loving words may be the nicest thing they hear all day—or even all week.

PROVERBS 4:23 – "Above all, be careful what you think, because your thoughts control your life."

Tuesday: Think of someone who you feel you have let down in some way, by breaking a promise, or not listening when then needed you, etc. Go to that person and apologize for what happened.

Wednesday: Who have you not spoken to in a while, perhaps someone you are annoyed with, or with whom you don't get along very well. Call that person and spend time sharing your life with him or her.

Thursday: Think about someone who you have judged harshly. Then get down on your knees and ask Jesus to forgive you for being unloving. Ask Him to help you change your thoughts so you are more accepting and loving of everyone.

PROVERBS 31:8 –   "Speak up for those who cannot speak for themselves, for the rights of all who are destitute."

Friday: Pray for courage to live your own faith conviction, even though it may be contrary to law or social norms. Pray fo and support those who are victims of unjust laws.

Saturday: Call or write the person on your list of people with whom you are not at ease (look back at your list from week four) —the one who you contacted before. Keep the love lines open. Pray that God will help you truly forgive any wrongs. Take the risk of sharing Jesus with that person.

PROVERBS 10:11 –   "The mouth of the righteous is a fountain of life, but the mouth of the wicked conceals violence."

LORD LET ME WALK
THE JOURNEY'S END – EASTER SUNDAY
The Year of Transformation: And a New Beginning

Our Lenten Journey has ended in triumph. The stone has been rolled away; the tomb is empty. Jesus has risen into the clear white Light of a new dawn, a new age, an age of Transformation. And with Him he takes our personal rainbows, glorious arcs of colors that in Him are balanced into perfect harmony.

Consider the nature of Light. It is the essence of Life. It brings with it warmth, hope, knowledge, growth, beauty and joy. All that has been hidden in darkness is revealed when light breaks through. The pain and despair in our hearts vanish, and we face the day with renewed hope and energy, strong and confident in our ability to create, accomplish and grow. Without light, there is no color, only monotonous shades of gray (try matching clothes in the dark!). Our hearts grow heavy, our bodies weary; our energy level drops and life feels dreary and dull. But when light banishes the darkness, everything is transformed: color streams everywhere we look, glowing, gorgeous and exuberant, lifting our hearts, lightening our load, encouraging us to live, to love, to laugh and to sing.

What happens when you hold a prism up to the light? It catches it and breaks it into its component parts—a Rainbow! Yes, our Lenten colors of red, orange, yellow, green, blue and purple, when balanced and blended together, transform into the pure white Light of Life. Only if the colors are in perfect balance will the transformation be complete and let the purity of white Light shine through. If any one color is out of balance, wider than the others, then that is the only color we see. If we are ruled by emotion, we radiate red; if pride owns us, others see only orange. And so on.

That is why it is vitally important to balance, with Jesus' help, the colors of our personal rainbows. Through our faith we have been baptized in Christ; through His death and resurrection, we have risen with Him into a new dawn, a new Light. Think of it: through Him, we have actually become human prisms. And when our colors are in perfect balance, we radiate out to the world the pure white Light of the risen Christ. In perfect balance, we transform into His vessels. In perfect balance, we become the Light illuminating the pathway to God, through Jesus. In perfect balance, there is no darkness, only pure, white Light.

Always remember: Life is a series of journeys. And the last step of each journey is merely the first step of the next one. Our Lenten Journey has ended; our Daily Journey has just begun. Each day, each month, will bring new challenges, new temptations, new opportunities. Our lives will bend and change as we continue to grow in God's love and walk in His footsteps.

And so the work of balancing our rainbow colors is an ongoing process. Each new event in our lives will uncover a hidden obstacle buried deep within that needs to be turned over to Jesus. Another color to rebalance; another harmony restored. As we continue our Journey With Jesus, working the steps faithfully, our lives will continue to transform. Each day our Light will shine a little clearer; each day our Light will glow a little brighter. And every day our hearts will beat more fully in tune with God's Love as we radiate God's pure Light out into the world for all to see.

Lord, Let Me Walk – The Journey Continues
Daily Balancing of Your Rainbow Colors Throughout the Year

THOUGHT FOR THE JOURNEY

"In the kind of world we have today, transformation might well be
our only real hope for survival."

~Stanislav Grof

MONDAYS: Make Mondays 'accept everyone' days. Make room
in your life for other ways of thinking and acting.

MONDAY PRAYER:
Lord Jesus, help me to love the way You loved all people, no
matter who they were, or what they had done. Please, Lord, help
me bring my red band of emotion into balance.

TUESDAYS: Take time on Tuesdays to thank others for the help
they've given you to grow and learn. Give credit to God for your
talents and abilities.

TUESDAY PRAYER:
Lord Jesus, help me to use my talents and abilities with humility,
to help and serve others in Your name.Please balance my orange
band of pride.

WEDNESDAYS: On Wednesdays, reach out and help someone you normally wouldn't even look at. Spend time with those less fortunate than yourself, just as Jesus did.

WEDNESDAY PRAYER:

Lord Jesus, help me to walk in Your shoes as you did. Help me to not be afraid of, or feel superior to, anyone else. Bring my yellow band of intellect into harmony.

THURSDAYS: Dedicate Thursdays to helping others. Do something for someone, anonymously. Only speak words of praise, comfort and encouragement today.

THURSDAY PRAYER:

Lord Jesus, help me be aware of others' needs, not just my own. Expand my green band of service so that I may truly serve You every day.

FRIDAYS: Make Fridays days of devotion—to God and to others. Volunteer at a soup kitchen; visit a sick friend; apologize for hurtful words or deeds.

FRIDAY PRAYER:

Lord Jesus, bring me closer into harmony with You and people of all nations. Stretch my blue band of spiritual devotion into true lovingkindness.

SATURDAYS: Make Saturdays 'Sonshine Days.' Share God's Love with everyone in thought, word and deed. Allow the transformation God is working in your life to be an inspiration to those around you. Let Jesus shine through in everything you do.

SATURDAY PRAYER:
Lord Jesus, use me as a conduit of your Love, Compassion and Service. Widen my purple band of majesty for the Glory of Your name.

SUNDAYS: Spend special time with God each Sunday, not just the time you spend in church. Make each Sunday a true Sabbath: read, meditate, pray, sing, dance—celebrate your relationship with God! And share that relationship with those around you.

Also, if you haven't yet, start a *Transformation Journal* and each Sunday note the changes that God is making in your life, the way your thoughts, words and deeds are becoming more Christ-like. What things did you used to say? How did you used to act? What has changed, and how?

Celebrate each step forward, even the baby steps. Look each week at who you were and who you are now becoming. Share those changes with the people around you.

ABOUT THE AUTHOR

Susan Grace O'Neill, a native of Buffalo, New York, and a life-long Catholic, has been active in her parish since she moved to the small California Central Coast town where she now resides. She works as the bookkeeper for a local monastery, and volunteers as the head of the music ministry for her local parish. She also sits on the Pastoral Council, and is a member of the Liturgy Committee.

Along with *Lord, Let Me Walk*, she has also written the first of six volumes of meditations on the Synoptic Parables: *Lord, Let Me Grow, A Journey With Jesus Through the Parables, Volume 1*. She is working on the next 5 volumes of that series, and beginning *Lord, Let Me Love: A Journey With Jesus to Calvary*, based on the Stations of the Cross.

Susan is also active in her local writing community. She belongs to SLO NightWriters and the local chapter of Sisters in Crime (SinC), where she served as president, treasurer, and newsletter editor for both organizations. She is also a member of SinC National and the Public Safety Writers Association (PSWA).

Under the name of Susan Tuttle, she has published four novels of suspense (*Tangled Webs; Proof of Identity; Piece By Piece; Sins of the Past)*, one novel of historical suspense, (*A Matter of Identity*, awarded 5 stars by Readers Favorite), and the first volume of a female PI series set in Los Osos, CA, *Tough Blood* (also awarded 5 stars by Readers Favorite). She has also published a 5-volume series of *Tiny Tales: 5-Minute or Less Reads for Busy People* books (Flash Fiction; Mystery/Suspense; Romancing the Muse; Scifi/Fantasy; Skylark, PI), a short story collection (*Death in the Valley*) and a book of poetry (*Mirror Eyes*), as well as a 6-volume workbook series on writing fiction and creative nonfiction (*Write It Right: Exercises to Unlock the Writer in Everyone*).

She also teaches weekly classes on writing fiction, and works as a freelance editor, speaker and presenter. She has won numerous awards for her writing at the Central Coast Writers Conference and other competitions, and her short pieces have appeared in five anthologies (*The Best of SLO NightWriters; Somewhere In Crime; Deadlines, Vol. 1; Deadlines, Vol. 2; Tales From A Rocky Coast, Vol. 1*). All of Susan's fiction books are available on Amazon and Kindle; her *Write It Right* series is available in print format from Amazon. Three of her novels are now available as audio books: *Proof of Identity, Sins of the Past,* and *Piece By Piece,* which should be available by July 2020, all narrated by Jan Kennedy.

For her secular writing, Susan is working on three stand-alone mystery novels, the next in the series that features Skylark, a female private investigator who has psychic abilities, two young adult fantasy series, and two adult fantasy series.

Susan lives with her imaginary cat in a house filled with her (mostly unfinished) handmade quilts and (mostly finished) knitted scarves. You can find her on Facebook (susanwriter), Twitter (stuttlewriter), LinkedIn, Goodreads, and you can keep up with her and read her blog on her website: www.SusanTuttleWrites.com. Her books can be found on her publisher's website: www.WriterWithinPubs.com.

This book is printed in Palatino type face,
in 13-point size for easier reading.

www.ingramcontent.com/pod-product-compliance
Lightning Source LLC
Chambersburg PA
CBHW081632040426
42449CB00014B/3278